MYSTERIOUS MICHIGAN

*The Lonely Ghost of Minnie Quay,
the Marvelous Manifestations
of Farmer Riley,
the Devil in Detroit and more*

AMBERROSE HAMMOND

THE
History
PRESS

Published by The History Press
Charleston, SC
www.historypress.com

First published 2022

Manufactured in the United States

ISBN 9781467149921

Library of Congress Control Number: 2022937899

For my wonderful mother and grandparents, who are always excited for everything I do, no matter how big or small. I love you.

CONTENTS

Acknowledgements   7
Introduction   9

PART ONE. SPEAKING WITH THE DEAD
1. The Rise of Spiritualism in Michigan   13
2. The Marvelous Manifestations of Farmer Riley   23
3. Choose Your Own Coffin   34
4. The "Devilish Cunningness" of Edward Ascher   41
5. Consulting Spirits: The Strange Finale of Eber B. Ward   53

PART TWO. LEGEND, LORE AND GHOSTS
6. The Legend of the Nain Rouge   73
7. The Lonely Ghost of Minnie Quay   82
8. Haunted Roads and Mysterious Lights   90
9. The Jackson Disturbance   95

PART THREE. THE STRANGE AND UNUSUAL
10. "Ye Shall See Strange Visions"   105
11. Driven Mad by Witchcraft   109
12. Frank Lesner, Witch Killer   112
13. The Devil in Detroit   120
14. The Summer of the Monster   128
15. The Mysterious Life and Times of Marian Spore Bush   134

Bibliography   149
About the Author   159

ACKNOWLEDGEMENTS

First and foremost, I'd like to acknowledge Kate Siebert Medicus, a librarian at Kent State University who photographed a frail and rare book for me and even followed up with the Ohio Historical Society to attain the last two pages missing from their copy. She was such an amazing help and a huge asset in my Farmer Riley research. Bryan Whitledge, an archivist from the Clarke Historical Library at Central Michigan University, scanned old Eber B. Ward documents. Thank you to my cemetery tour partner in crime and genealogy expert Jeanette Weiden at Loutit District Library, who always lends her knowledge and talents when I need it most. A special thanks to Blynne Olivieri, the head of Special Collections and an associate professor at West George University, for spending time going through boxes of William B. Roll's archived materials with me. I'd like to thank my wonderful library coworkers who allowed me to be flexible while working on this project and encouraged me along the way. I want to thank Scott Lambert for existing on the planet. Lastly, I would like to thank Julie Williams for listening, listening and listening some more.

INTRODUCTION

Welcome to the strange and unusual world of Michigan. When I was younger, I used to think this state was just the worst, with its long cold winters, brief mosquito-infested summers and lack of interesting history. In the fourth grade, we studied a children's textbook all about Michigan. We learned about the state animals, and I can't remember learning anything exciting beyond that. But when I started actively investigating the paranormal in 2000, a whole new and hidden world opened before me. I quickly left actual paranormal investigation (which consisted of going into people's homes or businesses in search of whatever spooky activity was pestering them) behind and became obsessed with the history behind ghost stories and hauntings. I enjoyed looking at why a place became haunted and tracing when and how the ghost story started. The more haunted Michigan history I searched for, the more wild and weird stories I found, and they weren't always about ghosts. Sometimes, they were just about an eccentric person, folklore and old legends, a monster, a forgotten crime or even the fascinating and tragic lives of nineteenth-century prostitutes, which I wrote about in my third book, *Wicked Grand Rapids*.

Many of the stories in this book are the products of me endlessly searching through old newspapers, periodicals and books in my free time for two decades. I included stories in this book that many people are probably not familiar with, but I included a few of my Michigan favorites, such as "The Lonely Ghost of Minnie Quay" and "The Legend of the Nain Rouge."

A *Detroit Free Press* illustration from July 22, 1928. © Detroit Free Press, *USA Today Network*.

For those already familiar with any of the stories, my goal was to add some details to the history that are not talked about or are often overlooked.

Michigan is no longer boring to me (but I still have a bone to pick with the winter), and I have many stories that are still waiting to find a home on the pages of a book. My two favorite people I wrote about for this project were Eber Brock Ward and Marian Spore Bush. I was curious if the famous Fox sisters of Spiritualism fame had ever toured Michigan and stumbled upon the fascinating battle over Eber's will. Marian Spore Bush appeared to me while researching mediumistic art, and I have been obsessively collecting information on both Eber and Marian since 2012. If I had a time machine, I'd go hang out with Marian in a heartbeat. So please enjoy these fascinating moments in Michigan's supernatural and mysterious past, and may you be inspired to go out in search of your own weird and wonderful history.

Part One

SPEAKING WITH THE DEAD

1

THE RISE OF SPIRITUALISM IN MICHIGAN

During the nineteenth century, nothing seemed impossible anymore. New discoveries and inventions were popping up everywhere. The Industrial Revolution of the 1840s and beyond was a powerful force, generating manufacturing and business faster than the world had ever seen. The field of science was improving the health and well-being of people globally with medical advancements such as vaccines for deadly diseases like smallpox, along with Louis Pasteur's 1861 germ theory, which extended the average human lifespan. Even the very foundation of human history and existence had a new challenger with Charles Darwin's 1859 theory of evolution, which shook the once solid ground of mainstream religion and invited people to question what they once believed to be true. However, Darwin, science and industrial progress weren't the only topics to shake things up in the nineteenth century. Two young girls living in Hydesville, New York, would become the catalyst behind the fastest-growing movement of the century—Spiritualism.

THE FOX SISTERS

In March 1848, sisters Margaretta (age fourteen) and Catherine Fox (age eleven, commonly known as Maggie and Kate) claimed to hear strange, disembodied rapping sounds inside their small home in Hydesville, New

MISS MARGARETTA FOX.   MISS CATHARINE FOX.   MRS FISH.

MRS. FISH AND THE MISSES FOX,
THE ORIGINAL MEDIUMS OF THE MYSTERIOUS NOISES AT ROCHESTER WESTERN, N. Y.

Margaretta and Catherine Fox with their older sister, Leah Fish. The print is from 1852. *Courtesy of the Library of Congress.*

York, just west of Rochester. The girls claimed the sounds responded to their questions—one rap for no, two for yes—and they eventually started to spell words. A spirit of a murdered peddler buried in the dirt cellar of the Fox home was the culprit behind the raps—or so the girls claimed. News of the mysterious communications spread fast. Neighbors and people from other towns gathered at the Fox home to witness the sounds for themselves. Questions were asked of the spirit, and the answers were declared truthful. Within just a few months, the sisters were a national (and eventually, an international) sensation that sent the world into a frenzy of spiritual communication. The sisters would go on to live somewhat tragic lives and would later be denounced as fakes. Skeptics believed the sisters made the sounds by snapping their joints in clever ways, which, at one point, they even admitted to, but frauds or not, what began with them grew into something larger. The idea that people could talk to the dead and receive advice and guidance become a core belief within what became known as the Spiritualism movement. Mediums, people who felt they were intermediaries between the land of the living and the dead, began popping up all over the United States to deliver messages of peace, comfort and sometimes deceit from the other side.

Spiritualists also came to believe that they were the one true "scientific" religion because mediums gave proof of the afterlife and could be "tested," and the scientific community actually took notice. The concept that a religion could be scientific became a unique aspect of Spiritualism that appealed to the progressive and intellectual minds of the day. The idea that paranormal phenomena could be studied, documented or debunked also led to the creation of research groups founded by brilliant men and women of the day. The Society for Psychical Research in Great Britain was founded in 1882, and a sister group, the American Society for Psychical Research, was founded by the father of psychology, William James, in 1884.

Spiritualism offered different things for different people. For some, it offered a much-needed assurance that bodily death was not the end. For others, it was a new way to express and exercise political beliefs and fight for the emerging social reforms of the era, such as women's suffrage and abolition. Many people who were attracted to Spiritualism were suffragettes, and from the beginning, the movement supported and encouraged women differently than other religions, even allowing women to lead their own congregations and speak behind the pulpit. Women found a new kind of empowerment in becoming Spiritualists or mediums. As a Spiritualist, a woman could have a voice with the help of the "other side." Author Molly

Mediums at the 1895 Vicksburg Spiritualist Camp at Fraser's Grove. *From the collection of the Kalamazoo Valley Museum.*

McGarry wrote, "As mediums, women were able to take center stage as public speakers; once there, they did not always confine their speech to spiritual matters." Mediumship was also a means by which women could work and be paid at a much higher rate than they usually received. While benefiting women, Spiritualism could also complement a person's existing religion. Many Christians adopted Spiritualist practices in addition to their established beliefs and felt it helped connect them to the afterlife and their loved ones who had passed on.

SPIRITUALISM IN MICHIGAN

Michigan was a fertile ground for the Spiritualism movement, particularly in the southwest part of the state and in the liberal and open-minded city of Battle Creek. Battle Creek became famous for introducing Americans to the concept of breakfast food and a healthy lifestyle, thanks to the eccentric John Kellogg and his Battle Creek health sanitarium that was inspired by the teachings of the Seventh-day Adventist Church, which was first established in Battle Creek in 1863. Battle Creek's progressive and liberal environment became a perfect place for alternative faiths to call home. Early settlers of Battle Creek migrated from what's known as the "burned-over district," an area of western New York that saw an explosion of new religious movements, such as Mormonism, Shakers, Millerism, the Oneida Society and Spiritualism. Quakers, another liberal group who were opposed to slavery and helped pave the way for the alternative spirituality that flourished in the area, settled in Battle Creek in the 1830s. By 1858, just ten years after the Fox sisters' famous "raps," Spiritualism had become firmly established in Battle Creek, and Southwest Michigan had become the Spiritualist capital of the Midwest.

The Ghost Town of Harmonia

Quakers who converted to Spiritualism became inspired to establish their own town with the pleasant name of Harmonia just six miles west of Battle Creek. The land was purchased by Reynolds and Dorcas Cornell in 1850 with the intention of creating a liberal utopia. The name was inspired by the book *The Great Harmonia* by Andrew Jackson Davis, who was known as the "Poughkeepsie Seer" and an early and major influence on Spiritualist doctrine. When Sojourner Truth, the famous abolitionist and women's rights activist, moved to Michigan, she bought a lot in Harmonia in 1857 and lived there for ten years before moving to Battle Creek. She never proclaimed herself to be a Spiritualist but identified with the Quakers who settled the area.

Ultimately, the dreams for Harmonia's ideal future did not play out as hoped. A tornado on August 4, 1862, ripped through the area, destroying homes and taking lives. Town founders Reynolds and Dorcas Cornell moved to Nebraska in 1863, which affected the town financially, and land surrounding the village was purchased for farmland, limiting the expansion of the town. During World War I in 1917, the land became a military camp called Camp Custer, which is now the Fort Custer Training Center. The only remaining physical trace of Harmonia is a cemetery with around seventy graves of the town's former citizens.

Spiritualist Camps and Organizations

Spiritualist camps were the predecessors of the modern-day paranormal conference. Mediums, lecturers, healers, believers and the curious could gather and spend days or weeks at any one of the camp locations around the state, which were usually set up around a lake or lovely park in the summer months for two to three weeks. A few camps that operated successfully for several years were set up in Grand Rapids at Briggs Park, Haslett Park near Lansing (now Lake Lansing Park), Island Lake at Brighton, Grand Ledge and the camp at Fraser's Grove in Vicksburg, which lasted the longest (from around 1883 to the early 1940s) and took place every August for a few weeks. The Vicksburg location was tucked away in a wooded area at the south end of the village on land owned by Jeannette Fraser. Author Arle Schneider wrote that it had been a dream of Fraser to open a "permanent metaphysical school" on her property, and by 1927, the camp had "evolved into the School of Devine Metaphysics and Psychology and was now a leading center in the middle west for instruction in metaphysics and applied psychology." Unfortunately, the school only lasted a year, as the founders were offered a better location in Indiana, and Fraser's Grove returned to being a Spiritualist camp. Even if the locals thought the Spiritualist camps were full of a bunch of "nuts," they were popular and drew large crowds that brought in substantial business for local merchants. The popularity of Spiritualism faded in the first half of the twentieth century, but the religion is still alive and well, with Spiritualist churches located all over Michigan and the United States. There are also a few permanent camps that are still operating, such as Lily Dale in Pomfret, New York; Camp Chesterfield in Chesterfield, Indiana; and Cassadaga Spiritualist Camp in Lake Helen, Florida.

Around the late 1990s through the 2000s, a new form of interest in the paranormal became popular—ghost hunting. Interest in the paranormal or making contact with the dead has always increased after national and global conflicts, such as the Civil War, both World War I and World War II and the events of September 11, 2001. Paranormal investigation groups formed all over the state and were looking to go "ghost hunting" or offer their services as paranormal investigators to homeowners and businesses. The rise in interest also coincided with the popular 2004 television show *Ghost Hunters*, which followed two men who were plumbers by day and ghost hunters by night into haunted locations. The paranormal reality show inspired people all over the United States to form paranormal teams and go in search of

A summer cabin at the 1895 Vicksburg Spiritualist Camp at Fraser's Grove. *From the collection of the Kalamazoo Valley Museum.*

The 1880 Vicksburg Spiritualist Camp at Fraser's Grove. *From the collection of the Kalamazoo Valley Museum.*

haunted locations in the hope of catching something on video, in pictures or on audio recordings. The fad came and went, with many of the groups in the state dissolving, but what this era brought about for Michigan was a sudden interest and awareness in the state's ghost lore and local history. Enthusiasts wanted to find haunted locations and began digging into their towns' histories for stories, unearthing forgotten and interesting information alongside documenting the paranormal experiences of fellow Michiganders. Many towns started to offer "ghost tours" of their historical locations and downtowns, and "paranormal tourism" became a niche market many have capitalized on successfully.

SPIRT COMMUNICATION FOR EVERYONE

The séance as we know it today, a group of people gathered around a table in total darkness or dimmed light, holding hands and asking for the spirits of the dead to return and give a message, came out of the Spiritualism movement. Many people who didn't follow Spiritualism as a religion still dabbled with its "tools of the trade" at home for fun or as something exciting to experiment with.

The talking board, or as it's more commonly known, the Ouija board, was developed in the latter half of the nineteenth century, during the height of the Spiritualism movement. A group of four businessmen saw money in mass production of the board and formed the Kennard Novelty Company in Baltimore, Maryland. They were granted a U.S. patent in 1891; the business dec'sion was a wild financial success and a major hit with the public. Marketed as just a mysterious tool that could make contact with spirits, the board appealed to people who didn't want to go to a medium or who didn't practice Spiritualism and were simply curious. Anyone could use it, and many did.

A wooden Ouija board that was produced between 1911 and 1914 by William Fuld. *Author's collection.*

The board continued to grow in popularity and showed no signs of stopping. Parker Brothers bought the game from then-owner William Fuld in 1966, and in 1967, the Ouija board outsold the company's most popular game, Monopoly. It wasn't until the 1973 release of the movie *The Exorcist*, in which the main character, Regan, plays with the board and gets herself possessed, that the board started to get a bad reputation as a doorway to hell or something "demonic." The board continues to either excite or terrify people to this day.

Ouija Madness in Michigan

The desire to communicate with the dead after the end of World War I brought on a wave of mass interest in the Ouija board. In Ann Arbor and among University of Michigan students, 1920 was a banner year for the Ouija board. Teachers were reporting that students' nerves "were shattered" by talking boards, claiming that the boards were becoming more common than Bibles. Two female students had allegedly left school to consult "nerve specialists" because of their "devotion to the Ouija board." In the fall of 1920, a local Ann Arbor store owner stated that he had sold more boards to students that year than he had in the past twenty-five years. Like little wooden predecessors to rock music, the Ouija board was rotting the minds of the youth, at least according to local spiritual leaders and adults. One student, after being told by the board that she would go to a dance with a certain man, used her entire savings to buy a new dress for the moment. With no money to get back home, she remained alone with her new dress at the school over Christmas and, in the end, was never invited to the dance by her crush. He came back from Christmas break with a new bride—so much for that advice.

The board became so popular that the *Jackson Citizen Patriot* sarcastically wrote, "Businessmen can hardly go to their work mornings without first consulting Ouija to see how the day is going to turn out

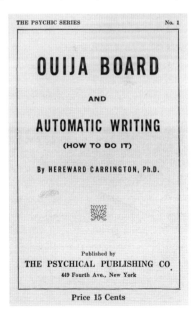

THE PSYCHIC SERIES — No. 1

OUIJA BOARD

AND

AUTOMATIC WRITING

(HOW TO DO IT)

By HEREWARD CARRINGTON, Ph.D.

Published by
THE PSYCHICAL PUBLISHING CO.
449 Fourth Ave., New York

Price 15 Cents

A Ouija board "how to" booklet from 1920. *Author's collection.*

in the stock markets. Dishes remain among the great unwashed while the once zealous housewife sits with her next-door neighbor and the cook asking questions of the Ouija board." In Jackson, a common question on the streets became "Do you Ouija?" *Ouija* had become a verb.

In Bay City, it was sweetly reported that Miss Genevieve Dolsen had a Ouija party on February 20, 1919. The news described it as an elegant tea party, writing that eighteen people had shown up for dancing, a "delicious buffet luncheon" and, obviously, communicating with the dead. The Ouija board is still a popular icon of the supernatural, and even if someone doesn't use it to communicate with the other side, they can buy the trademark Ouija logo and board on blankets, socks, coffee cups, shower curtains or doormats. It's safe to say that at over 130 years old, like it or not, the Ouija board has made an impact and is here to stay.

Stories from Michigan's Spiritualism Era

The nineteenth and early twentieth centuries of Michigan's Spiritualist era generated some fascinating stories and characters. The following tales offer a glimpse into this exciting and strange era, when it seemed like people could get away with almost anything and communication with the dead was as close as the nearest medium. The following stories look at the shadier side of the Spiritualism movement—rampant fraud. Nefarious men and women looking to make a quick dollar from people's grief devised all kinds of tricks, some that would impress the most competent magicians of their day. Like most things in history, it's the notorious stories that stand the test of time and still interest people many years later.

2

THE MARVELOUS MANIFESTATIONS OF FARMER RILEY

The key to being a great fraudulent medium in the nineteenth century was to establish a perfect reputation, put on a good show and never get caught. By all reports, the alleged mystical abilities of James "Farmer" Riley had even the most ardent skeptics scratching their heads. People doubting life beyond death came away believers after they witnessed the strange manifestations that materialized during his séances.

James Riley was a forty-eight-year-old farmer living in Marcellus, Michigan, in 1892 when stories of his talents began appearing in newspapers and Spiritualist periodicals. Séances at his home were given almost nightly with a waiting list of people from all over the United States. People wanted to know if the rumors of his uncanny powers were true, especially after stories spread that one could shake hands with the dead at Farmer Riley's place.

WHO WAS JAMES "FARMER" RILEY?

James Wesley Riley was born in Philadelphia on August 18, 1843. When he got into farming, his nickname "Farmer" stuck with him for life. James was the oldest of five children and lost his mother when he was only six. With no other options, his father left his children in the care of a neighbor and went to work in California for two years. The neighbor decided to move to Cass

County, Michigan, and had to take the Riley kids with them. By the age of thirteen, James had found work on farms and had become a well-known young man in the area.

With the start of the Civil War on April 12, 1861, just one day before his eighteenth birthday, James enlisted on August 17, 1861, and served for three years and eleven months in the 42nd Illinois Infantry, Company E. During the war, James saw horrible things and was involved in many of the largest battles, including the Siege of Corinth, Chickamauga and the fights at Shiloh and Stone River. During the Battle of Franklin in Tennessee, his friend John Boyd was shot between the eyes and died right next to him.

James was promoted to sergeant and returned home a few months after the end of the war on June 17, 1865. When he got back home, he married Martha Nichols, whom he had known since childhood. They settled on farmland in Marcellus and had seven children, of whom five survived into adulthood. He considered himself agnostic after his time spent in the war and the things he saw, but in the summer of 1885, a visit to a Spiritualist camp at Lake Cora in Paw Paw Township, Van Buren County, shook him to his core. Spiritualist camps were very popular around the state and typically featured lectures and demonstrations and were a place for mediums to ply their trade. He arrived at the camp with a chip on his shoulder and asked people to "point out a real medium" to him when they saw one. James saw all kinds of spirit demonstrations that day that were idiotic to him, but later in the evening, things would change for the stranger. A medium named Charles Barnes walked up to James with his eyes closed. Everyone assured him Charles was the real thing and that this was a "test" for James. Something was coming through Charles, and he had a message for James.

"Who are you?" James asked. Charles, still in some type of trance state, softly said, "I'm John Boyd." James was taken aback. It had been two decades since the end of the war, and he hadn't even thought of John recently, nor had he said anything about his old comrade and friend to anyone at the camp.

"If you're John Boyd, where were you shot?" James asked.

"Franklin, Tennessee," Charles said.

"Yes, but *where* about you were you shot?" pressed James.

"Right here, between the eyes." Charles placed his finger on his forehead where John was shot. Then the medium started to shuffle an invisible deck of cards. James and John always played cards during the war. James was shocked. He had been eating a meal, but his appetite was suddenly gone. He excused himself from the table and walked away from Charles Barnes and the so-called spirit of John Boyd with no logical explanation for what had taken place. That night set James on a path to learn what happened at Lake Cora and how such communication could come from a total stranger out of nowhere. It's not as if he was a total stranger to the ghostly. As a child, there were some odd moments he had no explanation for. He remembered playing with a little girl who would suddenly vanish up the chimney when his mother came into the room. As he got older, he wondered if she had just been a figment of his childhood imagination.

A portrait of James "Farmer" Riley. *Courtesy of the International Association for the Preservation of Spiritualist and Occult Periodicals, www.iapsop.com.*

James's wife, Martha, agreed to help him investigate mediumship, and they started to have a "sitting" every night at the kitchen table. They sometimes sat for hours, palms down on the table, meditating, clearing their minds and waiting for spirits to appear, sounds or the table to lift and tilt on its own. After six months, their efforts paid off, and like the Fox sisters before them, the first communications were raps. James claimed the table moved for them, tilting and tapping a table leg three times for "yes" and once for "no." The first spirit claimed to be Martha's brother Ezra, who died during the Civil War. One night later, James was reading at the table when the tablecloth began to flutter. James kept reading and passively said to his wife, "Martha, one of the children are hiding under the table." "That can't be. They are all here with me," she said from another room. James quickly lifted the tablecloth and peeking out at him was the face of the little ghost girl who used to play with him as a boy. She vanished, and he never saw her again. She appeared as if to let him know she hadn't been a figment of his imagination.

James claimed in 1886 to meet John Benton, his "spirit control." Spirit controls were highly developed souls whose purpose was to help develop a medium or help spirits come through during a séance. The belief in spirit controls was very popular among many nineteenth-century mediums, and almost every working medium claimed to be assisted by a spirit control. John Benton would remain a staple of Farmer Riley séances for the rest of his life.

James's abilities as a medium, thanks to John Benton, eventually developed into "physical mediumship." A physical medium was capable of producing spirit materializations that the living could see. He claimed he wasn't in favor of this at first, saying "the idea that he should be made the unconscious instrument of phenomena which he could not analyze was distasteful to him." But during a séance at his house, a "hand" materialized, waved to the circle of sitters and vanished, and that was just the beginning. Soon, full apparitions would appear like magic.

What Happens at a Riley Séance, Stays at the Riley Séance

Reports of what occurred during a Riley séance seemed too good to be true. Guests sometimes claimed to witness fifteen or more different spirits appear before their eyes, many of them recognizable as a great-aunt, a parent or a sibling. A celebrity would sometimes appear, such as a former president like Abraham Lincoln. But even more startling was how these spirits appeared. The forms would seem to build energy and rise from the floor until they became a full apparition, clear as day, and walk about the room, shake a hand or two and sometimes give a sitter a music box to hold or a fresh flower. When the spirits left, they would dematerialize in front of everyone, sometimes as if they were melting into the floor.

James would gather his guests in a crescent shape around a small bedroom doorway covered with black flannel curtains. The bedroom doubled as his "spirit cabinet," a nineteenth-century term for a place where mediums would retreat for privacy during a séance. In James's case, it was a spare bedroom, but they could also be small closet-like structures deliberately built for a medium to go inside; sometimes, they were just a curtained-off corner of a room or stage. The mysterious John Benton, always well dressed and very polite, would come out of the cabinet and address the sitters. He would also be the first to let people know when James needed a break or if the séance needed to end for the night.

Inside the bedroom, James sat in a chair next to the door and rested his forehead on the wall or in his hands and would go into a trance, becoming oblivious to the "wonders" that were taking place during a séance. The bedroom was sparsely decorated with two windows that were taped shut and covered so the room remained pitch black. His wife, Martha, also helped

The Riley Farmhouse. *Courtesy of the International Association for the Preservation of Spiritualist and Occult Periodicals, www.iapsop.com.*

manage séances, often guiding groups in songs that were believed to create the "right conditions" and bring a "harmonious accord" to the séances.

Before each séance, James and Martha would spend time talking to the guests. Refreshments and coffee would be available. Everyone spoke highly of the Riley family and thought they were good, down-to-earth people. James didn't even charge for his séances, but people would still leave him money as a donation for his time and their experience. James started to become one of the most celebrated mediums in Michigan and began making appearances at Spiritualist camps around the state and the country during the summer months. His first appearance was at the popular camp at Fraser's Grove in Vicksburg in August 1892. Reports claimed "Farmer" Riley was still able to perform his séance in public and wasn't confined to the use of his home. James had many supporters, but there were others who were not so quick to believe his abilities were genuine.

James let skeptical people inspect every room in his house thoroughly, even saying they could strip the home down to the studs if they put everything back together, just as it was. Sometimes, James would fill his hands with flour to prove he didn't move about the room during the séance. When checked, not a speck of flour would be found on the ground. The curtain was often pushed back during the séances to show him sitting in his chair, unmoved and in a trance.

Mendon resident Theodore Eveland's experience at Riley's appeared in the *Detroit Free Press* on July 5, 1893. Eveland showed up at James's house unannounced, but James kindly let him join the evening's circle. Everything occurred just as people said it would. Spirits materialized and slates delivered written messages, all in "good lamplight, not in the dark," another key part of James's séances that perplexed skeptics—they were never done in total darkness. Written spirit messages were delivered to sitters on small chalkboards called slates. The sound of chalk scribbling was often heard coming from the spirit cabinet. A ghostly hand, often "Mr. Benton's," would part the curtains and hand Martha the slate. Next came the actual spirits. "The spirits came from the cabinet in such rapid rotation that it would have been impossible for Riley to have changed his costume in such incredibly short time, much less to impersonate female characters as unlike him in feature and form as a gazelle differs from a billy goat," Eveland wrote. "Does anyone believe that Mr. Riley can keep twenty-five people employed night after night and pay them out of a mere pittance which he receives for his time—two dollars or three dollars at most?" he argued.

A reporter for the *Kalamazoo Gazette* disclosed his investigation on October 15, 1893, writing, "Every inch of the room [spirit cabinet], sides, ceiling and the floor, were carefully looked over, rubbed, dented and thumped till each particular skeptic seemed satisfied that all was right and really ashamed at their capaciousness, in light of the fact that the medium produces forms frequently and with the same facility in other houses."

During the séance, the reporter recognized his brother, who had died at the age of thirty-four, and wrote, "His first appearance was only momentary, the opening in the curtain exposing the form down about to the waist, then burst forth in full form from the curtain." The reporter's mother was with him, and his brother greeted her, shook her hand and nearly pulled her into the spirit cabinet until he let go of her hand, went into the curtain and melted into the floor. Another apparition appeared that was over six feet tall; it marched into the room and gave a woman a music box, and when it went back toward the curtain, instead of sinking into the floor, it appeared to be "melting upward and downward till all was consumed." So how was it that James Riley, a simple and aging farmer, was able to produce such an elaborate supernatural spectacle? Were people really seeing apparitions of the dead "melting upward and downward" as they materialized into our world and then back to theirs? Did James have some type of gift that was beyond what any other medium had?

FRIEND OR FAUX?

Other than the incredible witness testimony, opinions and experiences printed in newspapers and periodicals about Riley's séances, the personal details of James's life (whether true or false), such as how he became a medium, were recorded in two books: *The Mediumship of Farmer Riley* by Sydney Flower, published in 1900, and *The Life of James Riley* by Abraham Vlerebome, published in 1911. Sydney Flower, a somewhat shady personality from Chicago who was in the business of publishing periodicals on the emerging self-help philosophy branded as "New Thought," was highly skeptical of Spiritualism's mediums, which may have prompted him to investigate the much-talked-about James Riley. Sydney lived with James for two weeks and wanted to observe everything as a skeptic. James allowed Sydney to search every inch of his home and even sleep in the spare bedroom that served as the spirit cabinet. He wrote a fifty-eight-page booklet on his experience that included James's early life story and how he came into his mediumistic powers.

Oddly, Abraham Vlerebome's *The Life of James Riley*, published eleven years later, is almost entirely plagiarized from Flower's booklet, except where Vlerebome inserted his own thoughts and opinions on Spiritualism, the afterlife and some more recent positive testimony from James's believers. Vlerebome basically wrote himself as the one who had investigated and lived with Riley for two weeks. Perhaps James was hoping to have a best seller about his life and gave a copy of Flower's booklet to Vlerebome, telling him to just repeat what was written. Or maybe Sydney Flower didn't care and allowed them to use the material, but that's not known. The only thing Vlerebome didn't plagiarize was Sydney Flower's final thoughts about James, which were inconclusive. He seemed to be mixed on what the forms were and even suspected fraud at one point while sitting close to the spirit cabinet curtain during a séance. Doubts aside, Sydney couldn't emphasize enough how kind James and his family were to him. He actually felt bad that he couldn't write a book that settled once and for all that James was genuine. People didn't have a bad thing to say about James in the public media— except for Joseph Hagaman.

Hagaman lived in Adrian, Michigan, and was known as the "converted skeptic." He didn't like frauds and felt that many of the mediums were just that. While in Lansing in June 1894, Hagaman and some men went to a séance that was given by John F. Mabee, another "materializing medium" who had been frequenting the scene. During the séance, a spirit emerged and sat down to play the organ in the room, only to be attacked by Hagamen's group who found him to be "very much alive." Mabee was arrested for obtaining money under false pretenses.

Hagaman wrote in a letter published in the June 15, 1894, *Daily Telegram* that he had attended two séances of Farmer Riley's on May 26 and 27, 1894. After witnessing the forms appear, he wrote, "The manifestations represented as coming from the invisible world were so fraudulently presented that I did not think it worth the while to attempt a capture." He further wrote, "I publicly denounced Mr. Riley's manifestations as being fraudulent and gave him a challenge of $1,000 to sit for materialization under test conditions to prove his innocence, and his spiritual friends could not get him to accept the proposition." Hagaman even went as far as to accuse Riley of being a "saloon convict," saying, "You will find him in the saloon playing cards, etc., nearly every day of his life, and many people come to Marcellus and learn this and return home without further investigation."

TRICKS OF THE TRADE

In truth, James, much like many of the other "physical mediums" of his time, was really more of a talented magician than a conduit of the afterlife. Many things in James's séances pointed to signs of fraud, from the music box prop, the heavy black curtains, singing and slate-writing to James and his wife talking to guests beforehand. James and Martha would spend a long time talking to guests before séances and would learn all kinds of facts the people didn't realize they were supplying, such as where they were from, who they had lost or even an item they had that the spirit might recognize. Encouraging guests to sing, sometimes for fifteen minutes or more, easily blocked out the noises made by James or any of his assistants or "confederates" as they were commonly called if they had to move about. It's probable that James had at least one assistant in his "spirit control," John Benton. He also had adult children who could have been working behind the scenes. The sound of the music box was just another ploy to block out noises or direct the sitter's attention elsewhere for a while.

"Regulars" were said to always be at Riley's séances. It was a regular's job to sniff out any trouble, observe people's reactions or listen to conversations they could relay back. If information was gathered that someone was at the séance to expose it, or if someone spoke of grabbing one of the spirits,

James could then cut the séance short with the excuse that "the conditions were not right." James also said he could never manifest spirits during a thunderstorm, claiming the storm's energy affected his abilities. While a storm is the ultimate spooky background for a séance, lightning could easily brighten up a darkened room and expose the inner workings of the show, not to mention if any of his assistants had to come in and out of the house, rain wouldn't have benefited the production either. Sudden bursts of light were not something James wanted during his séance. A photographer from Kalamazoo came to multiple sittings at Riley's and finally asked if he could take a flash picture. Riley told the man John Benton would do his best to create a form that could handle the flash, but when the photograph was taken, James fell to the floor "knocked out" and was allegedly sick for days after the photograph. He had created a reason why there couldn't be any "flash photography" during his séances. But how did he create the famous forms that materialized and dematerialized right in front of people? How was it that people swore up and down that they were seeing multiple spirits and even recognized them?

Several books were written during Riley's time with the goal of exposing the frauds and educating the public. *Revelations of a Spirit Medium* was published in 1891, around the time Riley was starting his career. The author wished to remain anonymous, as he had been a fake medium for many years but wished to expose everything he had done. Many of the tricks James Riley used to his clever advantage were explained in the book, including the magical materialization of spirits. All someone needed to bring the dead back to life were some wigs, beards, masks, black cloth, gauze-like material, luminescent paint and, most importantly, a crowd of people with a "willingness to believe." The trick was executed by putting luminescent paint on parts of the clothing that would draw in the attention of the sitters. People would see something glowing appear out of nowhere in the dark or dim light, and their eyes would focus on it, believing it to be a spirit starting to form. Saturating large amounts of gauze-like material in the paint could create an eerie effect. Even turning the paint into a powder and applying it on the skin made for a spooky glowing hand that would emerge from the spirit cabinet curtain.

To create the startling effect of "melting" that so many of Riley's fans spoke about, the "spirit" would cover themselves with a black cloth to completely conceal their body. To create the effect of emerging from the ground, a person would lie on the floor behind the curtain and begin to slowly push their head through the curtains, perhaps with something glowing

"Revelations of a Spirit Medium" from 1881. *Public domain.*

on parts of their face. The crowd would be mesmerized that something was happening and hoped a message was coming their way. The person would continue to slowly rise and start to release the black covering from around them, exposing their clothes. Sometimes, the slower they moved the better, because it created the belief that the "spirit" was building up the energy it needed to appear.

Once they had emerged from the cabinet, the light would often be turned up just a bit so the figure could be seen. Everyone would be blown away by what they had just witnessed, especially when the spirit started to shake hands with people and "felt so life-like." To "melt" back into the floor, the "spirit" would retreat toward the curtain. They would either retrieve the black cloth or another assistant would make sure they got it, and they would begin to cover themselves back up as the light was turned back down. As their body turned black, they would slowly lower themselves to the ground, giving off the effect that they were dissolving back into the ether. As for the many different faces and forms people would report seeing, wigs, beards and masks could easily be hidden within a woman's dress in the dim light, fake panels in chairs or anywhere else that was carefully camouflaged. In the dim light, a wig change or fake beard could give the appearance that an "entirely new" spirit had arrived once the person had swapped their attire. An adult could sink down to their knees to give the appearance of a child.

It sounds crude and simple to twenty-first-century minds, but when done by practiced and skilled people, the whole production could be quite startling, and given that the typical crowd that was gathered wanted nothing more than to see the dead return, they ate it up and believed what they were seeing. They went in with the belief that Riley was genuine with no reason to deceive them because they hadn't even paid, so why should they believe they had seen anything but real spirits? Also, by not charging money, Riley could avoid being arrested and convicted of collecting money under false pretenses if someone had publicly exposed him.

James Riley died from a stroke at the age of seventy-five on May 20, 1919. He finished out his life without ever being officially exposed or arrested. It was said that James Riley's mediumship got better with age, likely because he was able to fine-tune the act for twenty-seven years and maintain the rules of a good fake medium: keep a good reputation, never get caught and put on a show they'll never forget.

3

CHOOSE YOUR OWN COFFIN

In 1906, forty-five-year-old Margaret Spencer had been a professional spirit medium for a decade and had lived in Grand Rapids for twenty-seven years. Spencer and her husband owned the Majestic Hotel on West Bridge Street, where she conducted her business in a séance room on the fourth floor she called "Little Heaven." Margaret maintained a good reputation with the local Spiritualist church, which considered her talents to be the real thing and often held spirit circles in her séance room. But others who had received readings from her knew there was something off, and much to the shock and horror of Grand Rapids, people would soon learn just how "off" Margaret really was.

Addicted to Spirits

The death of Esther Bulman's husband at forty-nine years old left her sad and lonely. Rather than be alone, around 1902, she moved to Grand Rapids from Buffalo, New York, to be closer to her sister Emmie Elliott. With what money she had from a life insurance policy, she purchased a small house on Alpine Avenue in Grand Rapids, just a couple houses away from Emmie. Someone felt Esther could find comfort in the services of a medium and introduced her to Margaret Spencer.

For one dollar, Esther was led into a small room with a table and high-backed chairs. Margaret sat down, leaned back comfortably and said the Lord's Prayer, which Esther repeated. Then the medium closed her eyes and went into a trance, seemingly oblivious to the world. Disembodied voices came from all over the darkened room. Esther was impressed and started to come back daily, sometimes twice a day. Her initial curiosity turned into an obsession.

The first spirit voice to appear for Esther was that of Frank Ogden, who Margaret explained was the departed spirit of a former Grand Rapids citizen but had become her spirit guide on the other side. Frank brought forth the spirit of Esther's husband, John. He greeted his wife, but the voice didn't sound like her husband's. Esther was a little hard of hearing, so she didn't question it. After six months of continuous visits, in January 1906, things started to take a dramatic turn in the séance room. A new spirit was coming through to deliver an important message to Esther, and that special spirit was her guardian angel. The angel's voice sounded male and told her that death was near and that she was no longer in need of her earthly belongings. There were grand plans for her soul in heaven, and she was to "reign as a queen among the angels." Esther was stunned by the message. All she needed to do, the voice continued, was start bringing everything she owned to Margaret, as these items would travel with her to heaven. And bring everything she did—from fine jewelry and furniture to canned goods and bedsheets. She even wrapped some of the items in tissue paper and black silk because she was told "the angels' hands are soft" and can't touch anything rough. With each visit, the deep voice of the guardian angel continued to instruct her on what she was to bring or do next. Some things got very specific, such as paying a bill Margaret had on an expensive coat that was being held for her at a store. The spirits told her Margaret would appreciate it, and anything else she did for Margaret made the spirits very happy. But with her death coming soon, she needed to take the next step on her path to heaven—plan her funeral.

Escorted by Margaret, Esther perused the various coffins at the Chambers Undertaking Company, where she picked out the one she liked best with a matching death shroud. She chose an expensive casket that was heliotrope, a purplish-pink color. Claude Chambers, the store's owner, didn't think much of it because he had worked with people before who knew they were sick and wanted to plan a funeral their own way. Esther explained to him that her doctor had said she would die soon and feared that if she didn't plan her own funeral arrangements, her family would bury her cheaply and keep the rest of her money.

The guardian angel continued to instruct Esther about her upcoming life change. Next, it told her, "You must write a letter telling your sister of your plans to move on from this mortal world." Esther was advised to bring a bottle of rosewater and five ounces of morphine when she came for her next reading. Esther brought the items but could only acquire a small amount of morphine, nowhere near the requested five ounces. Under Margaret's guidance, she wrote a letter that read as follows:

> *My Dear Sister—I am going to my Heavenly Salvation. There is nobody to blame for this. It is my last request that my body lie just as it is; nobody will open it. My last wish, dear sister, do as I say. I want my body cremated. My sufferings were so great, all through now. I am going to my Everlasting Home.*

The rosewater and morphine needed to be "blessed" by the spirits, so Margaret took the items and said she needed to place them on her "spirit pillow" for one week. The rosewater was given back to Esther a week later with the instructions to drink it at home but to keep the bottle wrapped and not look at the contents. She was to simply drink the rosewater and morphine and throw the bottle away in her garden. Esther drank the special "blessed" water and shortly after became ill. As she felt the sickness come on, she threw away the note she had written to her sister Emmie, realizing then that if she read it, it would appear as a suicide note. A doctor was called after she became sick and unresponsive. She came back around, and a nurse, Celestia Bangle, was appointed to watch over her.

Meanwhile, her family had become fed up with Esther's behavior. Her brother-in-law George Elliott had started the paperwork to have her committed for insanity and told her "she had gone crazy over Spiritualism and that she had been defrauded of her possessions." Her sister had noticed Esther's things were disappearing from her home. Esther had also mortgaged her house for $600, per the advice of the spirits, and had given the money to Margaret to "hang on to," along with more valuable jewelry and even her husband's pocket watch. Mysteriously, Esther's sister received a copy of the suicide note in the mail, even though Esther had never sent it. The note was the final straw for the family, along with the sudden onset of illness. While Celestia watched over Esther, Margaret called on her favorite client to see how she was doing. Esther's doctor said he was the only person who could administer medicine to her to prevent further poisonings. Celestia foolishly left Margaret alone with Esther and even brought her a glass of water when Margaret asked for one. Esther drank that water and shortly after became sick again.

The police were contacted about the bizarre situation once the family was able to talk some sense into Esther. Celestia Bangle told Esther that Margaret had called her "crazy," which insulted her and sobered up her senses. Esther was starting to understand the danger of the situation she had put herself in. If her family hadn't stepped in, she literally would have been on her way to heaven just as the so-called spirits had told her. Now, she needed to get everything she had given to Margaret back.

Celestia accompanied Esther to a final séance, during which Esther demanded the "spirits" give her possessions and money back. When Margaret came out of her "trance," Esther looked her in the eyes and said, "You poisoned me and robbed me." Celestia recalled the room smelled strangely of chloroform—so much so that she had to cover her nose with her handkerchief. Esther had smelled it, too. Had Margaret been trying one last time to get rid of them both?

Unparalleled Case

When detectives arrived at the Majestic Hotel to arrest Margaret Spencer on January 28, 1906, they found her gathering all of Esther's things. Esther surprisingly recovered everything but claimed she was missing some money. Margaret admitted to spending some of it because she said Esther had told her she could. Once the story hit the newspapers, citizens were shocked, and the *Grand Rapids Press* said, "The case was unparalleled." Nothing seemed to match just how low and cruel Margaret Spencer was or how utterly foolish Esther Bolman appeared to be for believing the things she was told. Even the *Detroit Free Press* drew cartoons of Esther that mocked her ignorance. Margaret was arraigned on January 29, 1906, and charged with larceny for a total of $1,100.

The story caught the attention of women, who filled the courtroom at the start of the trial. Many felt sorry for Esther Bulman and were on her side. Maybe the idea of a sad, lonely widow trying to contact her dead husband and getting everything taken from her while doing so pulled at people's heartstrings. Esther recounted what she was told during the séances while she was on the witness stand. "We were to go floating out of that back door together and rise over the city within sight of all the people, and the Lord was to turn to me and hand me the wand of government, and I was to direct the destinies of the universe," Esther said. She truly believed she had a role to play in the second coming. "Do you blame me for wanting to die?" Esther asked. But she had been warned not to work with Margaret by people who had heard bad things about her or knew the readings were bogus. Esther told the press, "I always thought she had a cold look. I was advised not to go near her. It's a shame the way I've been treated by that woman. And she called *me* crazy. She is more crazy than I."

When asked why she believed everything that happened in the séance room, Esther claimed, "I was not out of my mind. I was hypnotized." Hypnotized or not, Esther was certainly a troubled woman, which Margaret saw and preyed on. Margaret's lawyers tried to say it was Esther who was insane, but two doctors examined her and determined she wasn't crazy but was just in a "highly nervous condition."

Celestia Bangle was called to testify during the trial and revealed she used to nurse in the family of George Thompson, a farmer who lived near Walker. George visited Margaret for readings and "became interested in a Spiritualistic gold mining scheme." He believed the spirits could give him the location of successful gold mines out west and was willing to invest $2,000 until "he was prevented by some cooler headed friend." It was Margaret Spencer who was going to benefit from the spiritual gold mining, not George. Celestia's testimony further proved that Margaret was not an honest medium. The local Spiritualists had already distanced themselves from her and decided to leave her fate in the hands of the courts. Even Margaret's husband, Richard, seemed to be shocked by his wife's outrageous scheme. He visited her while she was briefly behind bars before paying bail and questioned her sudden and desperate need for money. She claimed she needed new things for their hotel, like curtains, rugs and money to pay the bills. During the trial, Richard testified that he had heard a conversation between Esther and his wife the day before she was arrested. Esther asked Margaret if she had used any of the money she had given her. Margaret said she had but stated, "Didn't you say I could?" "Yes," replied Esther, "but if you don't give it all back, they are going to commit me to the asylum." Margaret's lawyer argued "that if the respondent never expected to regain possession of her money, then the act was not larceny, whatever fraudulent actions caused the delivery of the cash." Spencer's lawyer also argued that it wasn't larceny because Esther had given everything "freely" and, in the case of the missing money, told her to use some of it as needed; therefore, everything was really more of a misunderstanding than larceny or even attempted murder.

The trial felt like a complicated chore in which no one seemed to know how to expertly argue for their side. No one seemed to know how to approach

Illustrations making fun of poor Esther Bulman from the *Detroit Free Press*, 1906. © Detroit Free Press, *USA Today Network*.

the case, and it slowly dragged on until a jury, on October 3, 1906, couldn't agree, and the case was scheduled for a retrial. All the jury had to decide was if Margaret Spencer was guilty of larceny. Somehow, she escaped charges of trying to kill Esther and making it appear like a suicide.

On September 16, 1907, the prosecutor suggested the case be dismissed. Esther got remarried on May 16, 1907, to sixty-one-year-old Thomas Burns, and it was said she had a change of heart after her marriage and no longer wanted to press charges. The case was officially dropped from the court calendar on January 1, 1909. Esther Bulman had found some degree of happiness in her life again and wanted to leave the whole embarrassing affair behind her.

Margaret and her husband, Richard, divorced sometime after the debacle and sold the Majestic Hotel. Margaret moved to California and spent time at a health sanitarium before eventually remarrying and passing away at the age of eighty-five on November 18, 1945, in Los Angeles. It was a very anticlimactic ending to a spectacularly strange and over-the-top criminal case in the history of Grand Rapids.

4

THE "DEVILISH CUNNINGNESS" OF EDWARD ASCHER

It was just another lovely day on Thursday, August 18, 1898, until a corpse was pulled from the water at Belle Isle, an island park in the Detroit River. Renting boats was a popular pastime at Belle Isle, and the river had been full of people paddling about and enjoying the warm, fresh air. Around 5:30 p.m., two men rowing happened to notice something in the water that didn't look right. They maneuvered their boat closer and were horrified to find the head of a man sticking out of the water.

The police arrived quickly, but it was quite the struggle to pull the dead man from the water. Copper wire wrapped around his legs was also attached to two large rocks. It was obvious that whoever had killed the man hoped their victim would never return to the surface. Aside from a bruise on the side of the head, the body was in good condition and was sent off to the county coroner for an autopsy and, hopefully, an identification.

The Disappearance of Valmore Nichols

Pittsfield Township dairy farmer Valmore Nichols was reported missing by his wife, Alice, on August 10, 1898. She became worried after he never returned home from a short trip to Detroit. It wasn't like him, but then again, his recent behavior wasn't normal to her. Something didn't feel right, and Alice suspected Valmore's interest in visiting Spiritualist mediums had caused more harm than good to her husband of twenty-five years. Eight days after she had reported her husband missing, a knock on her front door brought two police officers with bad news. Her husband's body had been pulled from the Detroit River at Belle Isle, and they asked if there was anything she could tell them to help solve what was now a murder case.

She told them Valmore had been visiting various spirit mediums for advice. He came to believe that there were oil and mineral deposits on his property and that if he could just learn the whereabouts of them, he could get the big break he needed. The forty-nine-year-old farmer had been struggling to make property payments to his bank, and the detectives learned that Valmore had recently borrowed $255 from a friend to help pay off the interest on his farm but the bank said they never received a payment, and no money was found in Valmore's clothes after he was pulled from the water.

Alice shared that her husband had been wearing a strange pouch-like cloth belt around his waist—even to bed. The pouch was kept hidden under his clothes, but on August 3, after he had fallen asleep, Alice gently moved back the blankets and lifted his nightshirt. She ran her hands over it and

A typical day on the Detroit River at Belle Isle Park. This image is from 1900. *Courtesy of the Library of Congress.*

could feel coins inside. She figured it was some strange ritual a medium had told him to do that he was blindly following, hoping it would send a miracle his way. Alice also turned over letters her husband had received from a medium he had been working with. One of the letters contained the instructions and purpose of the odd coin belt, telling him to fill it with gold coins and not tell anyone of its existence. Another letter asked Valmore to collect every letter written between them and bring them with him when he next came to Detroit. Detectives felt they had found their suspect in the medium who signed his name "Robert Lang."

From Medium to Murder Suspect

Twenty-nine-year-old Edward Ascher had spent the last twelve years moving around the United States and at least the past four years swindling people as a fake medium under the alias "Robert Lang." He began in Denver, moved to St. Louis and then to Cincinnati. If one left their morals and good conscience at the door, what he did made easy and fast money, and if he got caught, all he had to do was skip town and move on to the next. No one was physically hurt; they were just out of money.

While Edward was living in Louisville, Kentucky, sixty-one-year-old Sabra Gates had been paying him three dollars (around one hundred dollars today) per séance. According to Gates's daughter, Edward had also been treating her health with restorative "magnetic water" that only people of his caliber could create. Sabra went catatonic on September 15, 1897. Doctors tried to revive her, but she passed away. Dr. Robert M. Pfeiffer couldn't help but notice the dark-haired and very handsome young man who was by Sabra's side but wasn't a relative. He learned it was her medium, "Robert Lang." The doctor instantly suspected the man had something to do with Sabra's death and that maybe the "magnetic water" had something dangerous in it. Dr. Pfeiffer claimed Sabra had died of cocaine poisoning.

Edward was arrested, but the police couldn't get him on anything substantial, and he was later released from custody. Cocaine was used in many medicines in the United States and was sold over the counter until 1914. Dr. Pfeiffer had been treating Sabra for kidney issues, and while it is possible that his medications were what killed her, he denied it. Edward left Louisville in a hurry and went back to his hometown of Detroit,

Michigan, and continued to look for more gullible people, which he found in Valmore Nichols.

Valmore had been working with a medium named Donovan, who had skipped town after getting exposed, so Edward Ascher, as "Medium Lang," swooped in like a vulture to finish cleaning the bones Donovan left behind. Valmore was known by the swindlers as an "an easy money chap" and did exactly what he was told. Valmore and Edward began a letter correspondence in which Edward would give him spirit advice or a long-distance séance. All Valmore and Edward had to do was agree to sit down on the same day and time. Money would be sent for the long-distance séance, and Edward would send back the answers he received.

Valmore would sometimes travel to Detroit for in-person séances and would meet "Robert Lang" at a Lafayette Street boardinghouse room he used as an office. Alice said her husband would return from these trips not feeling well. He would be tired, dizzy and dehydrated. The *Detroit Free Press* wrote, "Ascher had already begun to work the gold racket on Nichols, making it an imperative condition in the interests of the spirits that he should bring with him all the gold possible." The paper suggested that Ascher was making him sick when he didn't bring enough money with him, which "angered the spirits." Maybe Ascher was giving Valmore some of his famous "magnetic water," such as he gave the doomed Sabra Gates.

Ascher was also "developing" Valmore to become a medium himself— for another cost, of course. The development scam was one of the most popular and profitable tricks in the fake medium playbook. Edward had been "developing" Sabra back in Louisville, too. Give the person some lessons, and if they never turn into a medium, well, maybe they just weren't cut out to be one—or they just needed more lessons.

Detectives quickly learned that "Robert Lang" was Detroit native Edward Ascher. But with no direct evidence, aside from the fact Ascher had been swindling Valmore, detectives had to work fast and hard to find any detail they could. Edward admitted to police that he had seen Valmore on August 10 from 1:00 to 3:00 p.m. but claimed he had no idea where he went after they met.

Detroit Boat Club employees at Belle Isle who had worked on August 10 were questioned. Boathouse records showed Valmore had rented boat six at 7:45 p.m., but with ninety-eight boats rented that day, it was hard to remember specifics about anyone or if boat six had come back with only one occupant. They were not charged an extra fee, so that means the boat was used within the allotted one-hour time. Edwin F. Hulbert had canoed

A Detroit Boat Club image from 1917. *Courtesy of the Library of Congress.*

that day, and when shown a photograph of Valmore, he remembered seeing the "stout" man and his "sandy mustache." Edwin said he had been rowing with a "slender-built fellow" wearing a brown suit and a derby hat. When Edward was shown a picture of Edward Ascher, he shrugged and felt it could "maybe" be the same guy, but he wasn't sure. John Patterson owned a hardware store on Jefferson Avenue in Detroit and remembered selling thirty feet of copper wire like the pieces that were wrapped around Valmore's legs. The man who bought the wire wasn't a regular, and when he was shown Edward's photograph, the detectives got another shrug. John couldn't be positive that he was the man who bought the copper.

Detectives Larken and High found Edward at the Island Lake Spiritualist Camp in Brighton, where he was staying at the Island Lake Hotel, and after hours of questioning, Edward Ascher, for a second time in less than a year, was arrested on August 19, 1898, for murder.

Spiritualists at the camp declared the arrest a "persecution" of one of their own, and the *Jackson Citizen* wrote, "The feminine portion of the camp was not backward in expressing its belief that Lang was innocent and felt satisfied that he would soon be cleared of the charge on which he was arrested. Lang seems to have made a hit with the ladies." News reports were quick to describe how "dapper" and handsome Edward Ascher was, as if that made the murder even more shocking—that such a good-looking man was capable of such a cold and calculated crime.

Even the hotel manager Adam Brown tried to protect Edward by barring the detectives from getting to the second floor and threatening the men with a wooden club. Detective High pulled out his gun and pointed it at Adam, who quickly put down the club and let the men pass. As they dragged Edward from the hotel, Adam yelled to him, "Keep your mouth shut until you speak to a lawyer." Edward never hid the fact that he had seen Valmore Nichols on August 10, but he insisted he was innocent of the crime. Without a strong alibi, nothing was working in Edward's favor. On August 24, 1898, Edward was formally charged with the murder of Valmore C. Nichols.

MURDER TRIAL NUMBER ONE

The news of Valmore's devious murder had spread fast and made finding an impartial jury almost impossible, so the trial didn't begin until December 16, 1898. Detective Sadler (for the prosecution) gathered witnesses and even traveled around the United States, stopping in Louisville to get the particulars of the death of Sabra Gates and finding John Kuprion, who had been swindled out of sixty dollars by "Medium Lang." The Ascher trial was another blow to the Detroit Spiritualism community, which had recently seen a lot of fake mediums exposed. This left the people who practiced mediumship honestly experiencing a decrease in clients. Detroiters who enjoyed the comfort and advice of a medium didn't know who they could trust anymore. On the first day of the trial, Edward's parents, Simon and Bertha Ascher, sat behind their son with worry apparent on their faces, and Bertha wore a steady stream of tears on her cheeks. Edward's parents had no idea that their son had been a con man. Edward, on the other hand, sat emotionless and looked bored with the proceedings.

Edward's lawyer George Robinson knew the case was going to be hard to defend. Edward was a known charlatan, which didn't help his case much, but he simply could have been with the wrong person at the wrong time, and the real murderer could still have been out there. Robinson argued that his client was arrested because he "maybe looked like the guy" and was scamming him. Just because Edward had seen Valmore that day didn't mean he was guilty. Others saw Valmore that day, too, and hadn't been arrested for murder.

The Wayne County medical examiner did a chemical analysis of the fluid found in Valmore's stomach and determined there was no poison. Four ounces of fluid in his lungs led him to believe he had died by drowning. Valmore's head had also been hit with a blunt object, and that led the doctor to believe that's when Valmore's legs were bound with the weighted rocks and he was tossed into the Detroit River.

If looks could kill, Alice Nichols's icy gaze would have stopped Edward's heart in a second as she took the stand on Monday, December 19. Alice wept while she admitted her husband had been "investigating" Spiritualism since 1896 and testified about the letters she had found, the coin belt and how sick her husband always seemed to be when he came back from Detroit after seeing "Robert Lang." When John Patterson, the hardware store owner, testified on Tuesday, he claimed he had remembered Edward being in his store before and didn't recognize the actual man who had purchased the copper wire. Fred Clough, a telephone operator, testified that Valmore had made a call on August 10 and that a man with him did not fit the description of Edward Ascher. Attorney E.S. Grece, who had been at the Island Lake Hotel and camp while Edward was there, remembered him reading the news of Valmore's murder and telling him Valmore was a friend and that he hoped they could solve the crime.

On Thursday, December 22, George Robinson rested the case for the defense without having one witness on the stand, including Edward. The *Detroit Free Press* wrote, "A bombshell thrown in the courtroom could have caused no greater surprise." The courtroom was filled to max capacity that morning; many of the onlookers were women waiting for the handsome Edward to finally take the stand on his behalf. However, Edward and his lawyer did not feel the prosecution had proven anything; therefore, they didn't feel the need to put a witness on the stand. Or did they do this because there weren't any solid witnesses in support of Edward? Even his "sweetheart," seventeen-year-old Maude Schultz, whose family owned the boardinghouse he frequented, had to admit under oath that Edward wasn't at her family home the night of the murder like he had first told the detectives. Edward's lawyer George Robinson admitted his client was a liar and a thief, but those traits didn't necessarily make him a murderer. Judge Chapin, who was presiding over the case, was speechless when the defense rested and said, "This incident in a murder trial stands unprecedented. I never before saw a case where the defendant in a murder trial did not produce witnesses to testify in his behalf."

On December 24, the jury went into session at 3:47 p.m., coincidentally, the *Detroit Free Press* pointed out, the same time Valmore called and talked to his wife for the last time on August 10. The jury deliberated for hours, and Edward's normal calm and stoic expression started to crack and show stress. He seemed distracted as he spoke to reporters, and eventually, a few tears fell from his dark gray eyes. The jury took twenty-one hours to decide but couldn't arrive at a unanimous verdict. Ten men voted for conviction, and two voted for innocence. Back at the jail, a cheerful Edward Ascher acknowledged reporters with a "Merry Christmas," and with that, a second trial was scheduled by Edward's attorneys.

MURDER TRIAL NUMBER TWO…THREE…FOUR

Edward's second trial began four months later on April 12, 1899. His family added another lawyer, Thomas J. Niven, to the team, and the prosecution was ready to bring back many of the same witnesses and evidence from the first trial. Edward was his usual calm and collected self on the first day back in the courtroom, with the *Detroit Free Press* stating, "He appears to be no more concerned in the progress of the case than does the least interested spectator." The prosecution focused heavily on Edward's fake mediumship, often bringing up witnesses who made the courtroom laugh. Andrew Ziebold admitted to being conned by "Robert Lang" after he responded to one of his newspaper advertisements. Andrew's bike had been stolen, and he wondered if a medium could possibly locate it. He paid "Lang" and was asked to "write his questions down for the spirits"; Lang would then communicate with them and get answers. Andrew wrote a question down for his dead brother to answer. "And what did the answer say?" Edward's lawyer George Robinson asked.

"Ascher told me that he had a sitting with the note and that he couldn't get anything very satisfactory but that I would get my bicycle if I waited long enough."

"Did you wait long enough?" asked Robinson.

"I'm still waiting," Andrew responded, which sent the courtroom into fits of laughter. John Kuprion, the witness Detective Larkin had found in Louisville, traveled to Detroit to testify that "Lang" had stolen sixty dollars from him and also instructed him to make and wear a belt filled with gold coins. Kuprion had showed Edward the belt he made and briefly left the room. Later, when Kuprion started to suspect he had been swindled, he opened the belt and found the twelve five-dollar gold coins had been replaced with twelve nickels. Edward had swapped the coins during the moment Kuprion left him alone with the belt.

Alice Nichols and Maude Schultz, the "sweetheart," had to take the stand again and repeat their original testimonies. Maude told the jury she had last seen Edward at 6:00 p.m. the night of the murder and that he did not stay at the boardinghouse. Edward's stony face softened when she stepped into the witness box, tears streaming down her face and her body trembling. While she was on the stand, it was the only time Edward actually talked to his lawyers during the trial. Love letters that didn't come out in the first trial were read in court, and on them, he had signed his name "Robert Lang"—revealing he had even been misleading her about his real identity. But she still admitted to being in love with him. Maude was at the courthouse every day of the trial, waiting to blow Edward a kiss as he was hauled back to the jail each night.

Evidence that Valmore had also been poisoned was brought to the table when Frank B. Meade, a druggist, told the jury that he had sold arsenic to Edward sometime in August 1898, but he wasn't sure of the exact date. He was pretty sure Edward was the same man who had come into his store and made the purchase.

Derlin J. Westfall, a barkeep, remembered seeing Valmore in his establishment on August 10, the day of his murder, eating lunch with another man. He kept noticing the men because they were always whispering to each other, but like many of the other witnesses, when he saw Edward, he didn't think it was the same man he had seen with Valmore. Edward's mother, father, sister and brother-in-law all testified that Edward had been home on the night of August 10. Through family, it was also learned Ezekiel was Edward's real name, but he started to call himself Edward after being teased.

On April 20, Edward finally took a seat on the witness stand with a "sarcastic smile." The entire courtroom shifted closer to clearly see and hear what he was going to say, and people stood on chairs to get a good look. Without holding anything back about his shady past, he freely admitted to being a "liar, a cheat and a swindler, but not a murderer." He told the jury he charged Valmore one dollar per sitting. He admitted he stole sixty dollars from John Kuprion in Louisville and purchased a small amount of arsenic from the drugstore, but it was used to kill fleas on Mrs. Schultz's dog at the boardinghouse.

"You have robbed Nichols ever since you have known him, haven't you?" Prosecutor Frazer asked Edward.

"Well, no, I can't call it robbing. He was satisfied. He paid me for my advice and services."

"Then you don't think you were doing wrong in cheating him?"

"Well, I didn't put my hand in his pocket and take his money," Edward bluntly stated.

Both sides finally rested, and the jury spent ten hours deliberating. Edward didn't blink an eye at the verdict of "guilty." He would be spending the rest of his life at Jackson Prison. Everything that convicted Edward was circumstantial evidence, and even the *Detroit Free Press* wrote, "There was lacking in the trial of Ascher some things that were essential to the forging of an indestructible chain of evidence." But Edward's past misdeeds and lack of morals were too hard for any jury to ignore. Edward and his lawyers felt confident the supreme court would be his next move for freedom.

A third trial was scheduled for November 5, 1901, but the entire jury was dismissed after juror Henry G. Poupard got all the men drunk at the Hotel Normandie, where they were sequestered. Even the police officer charged with watching them had gotten drunk. Henry then proceeded to tell the drunken jury members that Edward wasn't guilty and that the detectives just wanted to see Ascher locked up. It was also revealed that Henry was indebted to Edward's brother Louis and probably pulled his stunt to get in Louis's good graces.

A fourth and final trial was scheduled for February 23, 1903. Edward continued to remain cool and calm as always. The same points were made, and many of the same witnesses were recalled—nothing explosive or new came out during the trial. The trials had cost the taxpayers $5,916.88 (around $185,000 today). The jury deliberated for thirty-five hours, and it was decided that Ascher was still guilty of first-degree murder.

Edward told reporters, "I am innocent of the crime with which I was charged. I could not kill a man. It is not in me. I am too chickenhearted. Besides, I had no reason to murder Nichols," he said with a half-smile. "He would have given me anything he had for the taking. I have been sufficiently punished in the last four or five years for what faking I did."

Edward's last resort was a pardon, and after a couple denials from the parole board, Edward was finally granted his freedom on December 31, 1910. Edward's brother Louis had political affiliations and helped re-elect Governor Warner with the expectation that Warner would "take a look at his brother's case." Alice Nichols was horrified that he had been released,

A vintage postcard of the Hotel Normandie in Detroit, circa the early 1900s. *Author's collection.*

and the public was shocked, knowing it was a political favor. But Warner said the jurors from the last trial admitted to him that they had voted wrongly and had said "guilty" just to get out of the space they had been in for thirty-five hours, as it had "become foul."

GUILTY? NOT GUILTY?

Edward was truly a man without a care for how his actions affected others, but had he been wrongly convicted? His defense team was never able to build a story around another suspect, but it was suggested early in the trial that Edward had to have help tying up and disposing of Valmore's body. It was theorized Valmore had been rowed to an area of Belle Isle referred to as "marsh end" that was away from the public eye. This area also had a break wall made of the same type of rocks that were tied to Valmore's legs. There, Valmore was brought ashore and possibly knocked out. That's when his money was stolen, his legs were bound and his body was thrown into the water. Or was it possible that someone else knew about the gullible Valmore and the money scheme Edward was running and quietly planned the murder, fully knowing that Edward would be suspect number one? Is it possible they coaxed Valmore out for a pleasant boat ride knowing he had a large amount of money on him? The speculation could go on and on if Edward was as innocent as he claimed to be.

After his release, Edward moved out west and married Helen Kinder on July 7, 1913, in Vancouver, Washington. Census records show he was then living in Portland, Oregon, and by 1917, the couple had moved to San Francisco. Helen died on June 20, 1917, at the age of twenty-nine, and after that, Edward just disappeared—which is probably how a con man like himself would have liked his story to end.

5

CONSULTING SPIRITS

THE STRANGE FINALE OF EBER B. WARD

Death comes for us all when it's least expected, and while it seemed everything Eber Brock Ward touched turned to gold, he was still on the same playing field of life as everyone else. On January 2, 1875, at the age of sixty-three, he died from a stroke on a cold Detroit sidewalk. Eber Ward wasn't just anyone either; he was Detroit's and Michigan's first millionaire, one of the richest men in the Midwest, and he had accrued a vast fortune as an early titan of industry during the latter half of the nineteenth century. The man was a business genius, involved in almost every profitable industry that helped usher in the Industrial Revolution—from mining, steel and shipping to railroads and lumber. At the time of his death, his fortune and assets were estimated to be worth around $120,000,000 by today's standards. As soon as news of his death reached his family, a battle started to brew. Just hours after their father's death, Eber's sons, Milton and Charles, were sitting down with lawyers to discuss what would happen next. This wasn't going to be a simple case of dividing a father's fortune per the wishes of his will.

Eber had divorced his first wife, Mary, and sixty days later, on March 11, 1869, married Catherine Lyon, a woman half his age, in Ashtabula, Ohio. The couple had two young children when Eber passed. Milton knew Catherine was going to fight for what he believed rightfully belonged to Eber's first family, but Milton felt he had the upper hand in contesting the will—Eber's love of Spiritualism, darkened séance rooms and mediums. For many years, Eber consulted with spirit mediums to help decide his next business moves. Maybe the savvy Eber Ward was on to something, given the vast amount of success he created, but Milton and his team of lawyers felt they could build a case around the validity of the will, a will that was possibly created by a man of "unsound mind" with the advice of the dead.

Much to his son's dissatisfaction, Eber's will left almost everything to his second wife, Catherine, including his valuable timberlands and mills in Ludington, Michigan, which were worth millions. What was most insulting to Milton and

A portrait of Eber Brock Ward. *Public domain.*

the rest of the family was that the small inheritance they were to receive was to be paid monthly via a trustee in the sum of $200 (around $5,000 today).

Eber Ward had struggled with how to divide his fortune when he passed on, which led him to update his will multiple times. Ideally, he would have loved to have left plenty for all his family to live comfortably on for the rest of their days, but he was a realist and knew the eccentric personalities and challenges of his adult children all too well. His biggest fear was that his sons would squander all the money he had worked so hard to earn. Try as he might to make successful businessmen of his sons, he never succeeded and always felt like he had failed them as a parent.

A Most Peculiar Trial

"The Great Trial," as the *Detroit Free Press* named it, began on September 21, 1875, much to the excitement of many Detroiters, who looked forward to hearing all the sordid details about the life of Detroit's richest family. Lawyers for the contestants were prepared to attack Ward's belief in Spiritualism and further planned to attack his reputation by showing he had a family history of "idiots and lunatics" and that Ward himself was "delusional" during the creation of his will, therefore rendering it null and void.

Eber's interest in Spiritualism was front and center on the first day of the trial. Wirt Dexter, a lawyer for the proponents, objected to the arguments he was hearing, stating to the jury, "This case stands before the court precisely as if Captain Ward was a Methodist, a Presbyterian or a Baptist, and the mere fact of his religious belief can have had no effect upon his testamentary capacity." This case was about to challenge the Detroit courtroom in a way no case ever had. How could one belief be less valid than another? Did asking for advice from spirits somehow differ from someone asking for advice through prayer?

In just a couple of days, the trial had become so popular that people were placing bets on its outcome, and the courtroom was packed with spectators. Detroiters stopped in during their lunch breaks and sat through entire sessions as if they were at the theater. The trial was a hot story on local front pages and in national news. Many of Eber's friends and business associates took to the witness stand and advocated positively for his mental state. His friend Allen A. Griffith told the court that he "thought Ward had brains enough to cope with the whole state of Michigan." The first two weeks of the trial heard testimony from trusted men Eber had worked with through the years and other business associates, but the most exciting and sensational witnesses—and the ones the public looked forward to hearing from the most—were the famous mediums in Ward's life, literal supernatural celebrities of their day.

HENRY SLADE

The first of Ward's mysterious mediums to take the stand was the famous Henry Slade, whom Ward had known for fifteen years and would visit when he was in New York City. Slade had lived in Albion, Michigan, from the 1850s through the 1860s, and the city had a large population of Spiritualists, which is probably what influenced Slade in his youth. Henry Slade became famous for slate-writing, which was a séance room trick he is credited with inventing. Slate-writing was the belief that spirits left written messages on ordinary, small chalkboards. The trick was nothing more than sleight-of-hand, and a year later, on October 1, 1876, Henry would be tried and convicted of fraud in London and sentenced to three months in prison, only to get off on a technicality and never serve time. He would continue to be caught in the act of fraud for the rest of his life but never gave up his profession.

From the start of the trial, Milton's lawyers consistently branded Spiritualism as a "delusion." Proponent lawyer Wirt Dexter used this to his advantage and argued that Slade's testimony should be thrown out, because "if people believing in Spiritualism are 'delusional,' then Slade cannot be a reliable witness to testify, because his belief in Spiritualism would render him delusional as well." The courtroom spectators clapped loudly after Dexter's smart yet sarcastic observation.

Judge Patchin allowed Slade's testimony, and he told details of their séance sittings, remembering, in 1873, one of his spirit slates declaring "there was hereditary insanity" in Ward's family and to make sure his finances were in order so his children didn't "squander" his money. Suspiciously, the message stated that Eber's wife, Catherine, was perfectly capable of handling the fortune herself and that it would be best

A portrait of Henry Slade. *Public domain.*

to leave the Ludington lumber business to her. The spirits supplying this advice were said to be relatives of Catherine's who were looking out for her. Slade remembered Ward taking notes during the session so he could compare them to what other mediums said. Catherine traveled with her husband to New York City many times and had sometimes gone with him to séances but claimed she didn't know Henry Slade personally. Contestant lawyer Theodore Romeyn theorized that Catherine could have secretly contacted Slade to get him to plant messages of her own design when Eber visited. He was most likely on to something, given that Slade was in fact a fraud. J. Irvine Crabbe, who did busy work and ran errands for Ward and often traveled with him, was very familiar with Ward's love of mediums. Crabbe accompanied Eber and Catherine to New York City, where they visited Charles Foster, a medium and a friend of Henry Slade. Crabbe told the courtroom he was alarmed when, very casually, Foster said, "Kate, you sit here," at the start of the séance, using her first name as if he had known her for years. Catherine immediately chastised Foster for not addressing her properly, but Crabbe said the two seemed familiar with each other.

Was Catherine behind some of the messages Eber received? Was she manipulating her husband through spirit mediums? It wouldn't have been difficult to deliver a message or make a personal visit to Eber's favorite mediums. She could have paid the person handsomely to give her husband the advice she wanted him to receive from the spirits, especially when Eber asked the spirits to advise him on his will. Allen A. Griffith, a friend of Ward's, went to several séances with him, including one given by Henry Slade.

Sitting around the darkened séance table, Griffith immediately recognized fraud taking place and told Eber what he thought, but Eber "insisted that the manifestations were the result of spirit agencies."

SARAH CARTWRIGHT

Eber Ward and Michigan senator Jacob M. Howard had known each other for many years and were good friends. They held similar political beliefs and supported abolition, with Howard helping Abraham Lincoln draft the Thirteenth Amendment of the U.S. Constitution. Howard passed away on April 2, 1871. Aware that fraud was common in the business of mediumship, Ward considered himself an "investigator" of Spiritualism, not necessarily a full-blown believer, and he would give the mediums tests to decide if they were genuine in his mind. When he first met clairvoyant medium Sarah Cartwright, he handed her a piece of hair and asked her who it belonged to. She held it and closed her eyes. "It belonged to a prisoner," she told him. Eber was happy with her answer and continued to use her services.

Sarah told the court about her séances with Eber and remembered Senator Howard's spirit coming through often. As another test, Ward asked Sarah to tell him the last thing he and Jacob Howard had talked about before he died. She told him, "The Burlington railroad," which was correct—another test passed. Howard eventually brought an ominous message though. He told Eber his death wasn't far off, and worried, Eber asked his old friend what he should do with his wealth and property. Sarah Cartwright wasn't a flashy medium. She didn't advertise her services and didn't use gimmicks or darkened séance rooms. As a clairvoyant, she claimed she just saw something in her mind's eye and relayed the message. Sarah remembered Catherine being at one of her séances when she had a vision of a man killed after falling from a wagon. Catherine

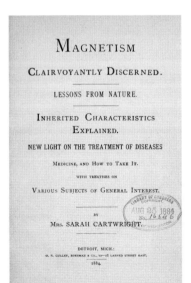

The title page of Sarah Cartwright's book about her beliefs and practices. *Public domain.*

spoke up and said that was how her father had died. Impressed by her ability, Catherine rather suspiciously asked Sarah how long Eber was going to live and if his unstable son Henry would ever be a danger to the family. In 1874, Sarah recalled Eber asking the spirit of Senator Howard if there were going to be problems between the families of his first and second marriages. Eber's first wife, Mary, whom he always called Polly, came through Sarah and sternly warned, "Don't you do any injustice to my children."

"What ought I to do?" Eber asked her.

"Do what your heart dictates," she said. Frustrated with the vague answer, Eber threw his arms up and said, "Oh, you and I never could agree." When Eber left Sarah's that day, he shook her hand, which, the *Detroit Free Press* pointed out, was a "very unusual thing for him to do."

THOSE FAMOUS FOX SISTERS

The air in the courtroom was buzzing with excitement on September 30, 1875, when Margaretta "Maggie" Fox, one of the celebrated Fox sisters and unintentional founders of Spiritualism, stepped into the witness box. Sitting in front of the spectators was one of the young girls who, in 1848, had sent the world into a frenzy of spirit communication after insisting they had established a dialogue with spirits through a system of rapping sounds. Maggie Fox was then forty-two years old and widowed after a short marriage to Elisha Kent Cane, the American explorer who died in 1857 in Cuba after an illness.

Maggie took her oath and said she had known Eber for around eight years and had been a frequent guest at her New York City séance parlor. She was described as a "writing medium" who wrote down the spectral messages she received. She would sometimes use both hands simultaneously to record the messages that allegedly came through her. Maggie said Eber had come to see her in the spring of 1874 because his wife, Catherine, was not happy with his current will and he needed guidance. Maggie summoned up the spirits, and another revision of Eber's will was created. Maggie was asked to show the court these "spirit dictated" documents she wrote. She read what appeared to be a perfectly executed will dictated, not by Catherine's ghostly relatives this time, but by the spirit of Ward's first wife, Mary. It said everything should be divided equally. Yet another document she had with her stated the complete opposite, specifically saying, "Give Cate L., your wife, all the pinelands and sawmills, and everything to carry on the lumber business, free from debt." When Maggie was asked if she had ever had any contact with Eber's wife, Catherine, she said she hadn't. Milton was the one who contacted her to come to testify, but it was evident that Milton, Catherine or both of them had possibly been paying her to give the advice they wanted Eber to hear. She claimed to not really know Henry Slade, having only met him once in New York City, and the second time they met was at the trial in Detroit. The trial was becoming a spectacle, but the strangest witness was yet to come.

And then Things Got Weird...

The courtroom wasn't prepared for the strange scene that unfolded while thirty-four-year-old Detroit trance medium Emma Martin was on the stand. Trance mediums believed spirits could speak through them while they slipped into a trance-like state. Emma claimed to channel the spirit of a German geologist nicknamed "Cabbage John," whom Eber relied heavily on for business advice, especially regarding his mining business. When Emma expressed a desire to move to California, Eber offered to build her a home on Sixteenth Street in Detroit, not far from his opulent Fort Street mansion, and pay her better than what the Spiritualist lecture circuit and patrons would. He felt her services were too valuable for her to move away from him. There were even rumors that she was his "mistress," which she was aware of but said were false.

To prove or disprove Emma's otherworldly connections, proponent lawyer Ashley Pond asked Emma if she could demonstrate her abilities to the court. "Yes, sir," she said with confidence. The courtroom went dead silent, and reporters crept a little closer to the witness box. The *Detroit Free Press* wrote, "In about half a minute, her body was seen to jerk spasmodically; her lips trembled visibly." She paused for a while and then said in German, "Who will speak with me?" Everyone remained wide-eyed and silent, even the lawyers. "Who will speak with me?" she repeated. Her voice was altered and lower. Judge Patchin told a slack-jawed Ashley Pond that Emma was his witness and, "whether ghost or human," to get on with the questioning. Unsure of what to do, Pond awkwardly asked, "What is your name?" Emma didn't respond until the stenographer repeated the question in German.

"Andrew Kurthaldrus," Emma responded. Half in English and half in "bad German," Emma mumbled something about no one wanting to speak to the spirit. No one in the courtroom seemed eager to volunteer. Emma's body jerked back to Earth. She opened her eyes and looked around, slightly confused, claiming to have no memory of what had just transpired. The court appeared genuinely spooked by the event, with reports later saying her face took on a rather eerie transformation that did "look decidedly Teutonic."

What was most chilling wasn't Emma's spectral transformation but a piece of testimony that possibly proved how much Eber was being manipulated by humans—not spirits. Emma stated that a man named McConnel offered her $25,000 if she would tell Eber to buy a mine in Utah. She said she denied him and told Eber all about the bribe. This piece of testimony solidified the theory that interested persons were supplying Eber's mediums with the advice they wanted him to hear.

THE FINAL DAYS OF THE "GREAT TRIAL"

The entertainment value of the trial waxed and waned as the days turned into weeks and the witnesses became mundane, everyday people, not mystical mediums with supernatural abilities. The battle of proving their father to be "of unsound mind" was a constant focus for the contestants, but no witness for either side seemed to feel Eber was an incapable man, even after a previous stroke in 1869. He recovered from that stroke, but those who knew him well admitted he was a little slower after that—perhaps not as sharp but not insane by any definition of the word. Three weeks into the trial, the final witnesses to revive public interest were Milton and Emily Ward.

Eber's older sister Emily was one of Eber's closest confidants, and his respect for her was infinite. After the death of their mother, ten-year-old Emily helped raise her three siblings, Sallie, Abbie and the youngest, Eber. When Eber built a new Fort Street mansion after his second marriage, right across the street from his first mansion, he gladly gave the extra mansion to his sister. Emily was affectionately known as "Aunt Emily" by everyone and was a strong-minded woman who never married. "I didn't have time to get married," she said, because she was "married" to her philanthropy work with orphaned children. Emily raised fourteen orphaned children

An engraving of Emily Ward. *Public domain.*

to become successful men and women. The September 1891 *Religio-Philosophical Journal* wrote, "Had she been a man, she would have equaled her brother, Eber, in the business world, and she surpassed him in philanthropic endeavor."

Eber's children were always a topic of concern between Emily and her brother. As a young child, Milton had a temper and the "inability to keep at one particular thing," which would be diagnosed today as attention deficit disorder. Milton was often sent to his aunt's when he was acting up, and Emily recalled "he never seemed satisfied anywhere." It is apparent through Emily's testimony that she wasn't fond of Milton and considered him to be arrogant and a drunk. Eber had once told Emily that "Milton was extravagant in almost everything he touched in his life and habits and conversation." While in the witness box, Emily seemed evasive when proponent lawyer Theodore Romeyn asked her, "Do you remember saying that Captain Ward was like dough in the hands of Mrs. Ward?" "I say that of every man who has a wife," she said, and the courtroom burst into laughter.

Milton sat down in the witness chair on October 20, 1875. He largely tried to defend himself about his entitled behavior, drunkenness and lack of work ethic, claiming he rarely touched alcohol. Spectators seemed mildly entertained by Milton, who was often frank about his life and sometimes humorous. He talked about his childhood and how he had been shuffled around to different private schools to try to paint himself in a sympathetic light. He readily admitted to some of the rumors about him, such as throwing a knife at his housekeeper Mary Brindle because he had wanted coffee but "could only get slops." When Milton complained to her, he said she "intimated that the world was wide, and if I didn't like it, I could get out. I replied by throwing a case knife or a fork, I don't remember which, at her." He justified the action by saying he had been sick for ten days. The rest of his testimony tried to justify why he had failed at every job his father had given to him.

On November 12, 1875, both sides had finally rested their case, and it was up to the jury to decide whether "the will in question either is or is not the will of the testator." The jury deliberated for fifty-four hours, and after months of excitement and bets placed, the jury could not unanimously agree on a verdict. Eight jury members were for the contestants, and four were for the proponents. A second trial was scheduled for March 7, 1876, but not wanting to go through the process again, the two sides came to an agreement. Catherine and her children would get the Ludington property, and the rest of the estate went to Eber's first family and his sister, Emily. The $200-a-month allowance was annulled. Catherine Ward became one of the richest women in the Midwest.

The Family Tragedies

Eber had eight children with his first wife, Mary Margaret McQueen, whom he married in 1837. Their children were named John, Samuel, Elizabeth, Henry, Milton, Charles, Fred and Mary. Samuel died at only three months old in 1845. While much of Eber's life was filled with success, it was also periodically afflicted with tragedy. It would seem like a blessing to be born and raised in one of the richest households in the Midwest, but wealth aside, Ward's children had their own personal demons to contend with.

A Son Murdered

The first major tragedy that would befall the family happened to Eber's oldest son, John Pray Ward, who was murdered at the age of twenty-seven. A ship captain, John had become successful in Great Lakes shipping and had built a small fortune for himself, but one awful decision would change everything. A September 13, 1865, article from the *Detroit Free Press* reported the story of John wooing a young girl while she traveled aboard the steamer *Forester*. As the ship's captain, he invited the girl and her friend to a private dinner; allegedly gave them champagne, according to one story; and took a liking to one of the girls named Ida Farman. He invited her to walk with him on the upper deck of the ship, where he sexually assaulted her. Back home in Lexington, Michigan, Ida told her mother what had happened, and the police were notified. The poor girl was just a few weeks shy of fifteen but was described as intellectually behind other girls her age.

John didn't deny that he had had sexual relations with the young girl, even though he was recently married on May 10, 1865, and had a baby on the way. In his defense, he said that Ida was a willing partner and had actually seduced him. Knowing whose son he was, John claimed she attempted to blackmail him for money, saying she would go to the police with their affair if he didn't pay—or so John said.

John was arrested and put in jail in Lexington but paid the bail of $7,500. It was rumored that Ida was offered money by the powerful Ward family to step back and allow John to walk free. Ida's father had died some years prior, and the family was poor, but if the Ward bribery story was true, they never took the money. A month later, John was still set to be tried, and on Friday, October 13, 1865, the day would live up to its unlucky reputation for Captain John P. Ward.

Ida had given her heartbreaking testimony that day in the Lexington courtroom, and none of the witnesses called had one damaging word to say about her or her reputation. The evidence was against John P. Ward, but it was possible he could still walk away unpunished. During the trial, Ida's sixteen-year-old brother, Frederick, sat in the room, glaring at John to the point that he became uncomfortable with the young man's cold stare. At 9:00 p.m., the court was adjourned. As John and a couple of friends left the courtroom, Frederick followed, and at about one hundred yards, he aimed a pistol at John's back and fired. John staggered and fell to the ground. Frederick fired two more shots into him. With vengeance achieved, he willingly let himself be arrested and handed over the gun without a fight, saying, "I have no more need of it now."

John's bullet wounds were fatal, one having severed his spinal cord. Eber Ward brought his injured son home to Detroit, where he died nine days later on October 22. The story garnered considerable attention, given the high social status of the Ward family, but people were sympathetic to the Farman family and Frederick's act of vigilantism. Frederick firmly believed that the captain was going to go unpunished and, taking matters into his own hands, made sure he would pay for what he did, no matter what a jury decided. A murder trial for Frederick didn't take place until November 1867, largely because securing impartial jury members who hadn't heard the story was difficult. At the end of the trial, the jury could not arrive at a consensus. Eight jurors were for conviction, and four were for acquittal. The case was abandoned.

More Family Struggles

Talk of hereditary insanity in Eber Ward's family history and children was the topic of gossip well before Eber's death. The Ward children grew up with everything they could ever want, and that showed in the everyday behaviors of his sons. Eber tried to turn his sons, namely Milton and Charles, into hardworking men who could steer his empire into the future. He tried to inspire a good work ethic in them by allowing them to indulge in their interests. Charles wanted to learn chemistry, so Eber built him a complete lab to tinker in, feeling Charles could learn to test the purity of minerals from his mine investments, but Charles's interest was fleeting. Charles thought he had a better way to make a boat, and even though Eber disagreed with his idea, he bought him all the materials he needed to build a boat. After the boat was finished, something was off in its balance, and when they launched it into the water, it tipped—so much for that hobby.

Eber had also secured a lucrative position for Charles with the Second National Bank of Detroit, but Charles spent every penny he made from the job and more. Ward complained that Charles "had no comprehension of the value of money." Eber had given Charles $1,800 (around $33,000 today), and it was gone in eight months. His paycheck was spent as soon as he got it. Eber even had to pay debts in Charles's name off frequently.

Milton worked in Ludington for a time, managing and overseeing the building of a sawmill, but he was miserable and became convinced the other workers were deliberately setting him up to fail because of whose son he was. He left Ludington in April 1873, after contracting malaria. Earlier, Milton had worked on property the family owned in Ohio that they called "The Black Swamp," and there he lost money for his father.

After the trial was over, Milton didn't stay in Detroit. He moved to New Jersey and then in the fall of 1877, he went to Mobile, Alabama, and then on to the West Indies. He died from an illness at the age of twenty-seven in Kingston, Jamaica, on May 26, 1877, just a little over a year and a half after the trial was finished. No one back in Detroit even knew he had died until July 31, and his body was never shipped back to be buried in the Ward family lot in Elmwood Cemetery, per his wishes.

Henry Ward was easily aggravated and quick to pull his pistol and wave it about when he got upset. During the trial, Henry became so upset over something lawyer Wirt Dexter said about his mother that he lunged at him, screaming he would "blow his head off." Henry was held back, and a police officer escorted him from the courtroom. The *Detroit Free Press* wrote that Henry was "particularly susceptible to excitement."

One afternoon during lunch at the Fort Street Ward mansion, Henry had proclaimed himself a spiritual medium, and Milton told him, "He was no more a medium than an old cat," which set Henry off. Out came his pistol, which sent Milton into a rage. Milton grabbed a carving knife from the table and chased him around the dining room with it, threatening to kill him. Emily Ward had witnessed this scene and told the courtroom about it during her testimony. Henry was never married but had two illegitimate children. He spent time in and out of asylums and died at the age of forty-nine at the Kalamazoo Asylum for Insanity from a stroke.

At the age of nineteen, Frederick Ward overdosed on laudanum, something he had formed a habit of consuming along with alcohol. Frederick had already spent time at Binghamton in New York, an "inebriate asylum" that he asked to be sent to. It was the first hospital of its kind that treated alcoholism as a mental disorder. Eber had even offered him money to stop drinking, but no amount of money could cure Frederick of his depression. A large painting of a flower wreath that hung in Eber's library was also the cause of considerable grief for the family and Frederick. The painting was done by Mrs. A.E. Blair, a one-armed spirit medium who painted while thickly blindfolded. Each flower in the wreath was supposed to represent relatives, both dead and living, even though she allegedly didn't know anything about the people she painted for. Frederick was the only person not represented in the painting. Eber had always doubted that Frederick was his biological child. Emily Ward was also aware that her brother held this belief, possibly suggesting his first wife, Mary, had a relationship outside of the marriage. Not feeling like part of the family may have contributed to Frederick's mental health problems. Emily Ward was at Frederick's side when the young man took his last breath.

Eber's daughters Mary and Elizabeth had the least drama, but Elizabeth was considered "mentally incompetent" and needed a caretaker. It's hard to say what her condition was, but she was not able to care for herself. A probate record from 1893 shows an application to send her to Oak Grove Sanitarium in Flint, which was an exclusive hospital for wealthy people with mental health issues or addictions. She lived to be seventy-eight years old and died on November 4, 1924. Mary Ward, who was just considered "eccentric," married William B. Ely on November 28, 1876, but died after childbirth on May 11, 1879, around the age of twenty-three. William died from pneumonia one year later to the day on May 11, 1880, at the age of twenty-five. During the trial, it came out that Catherine had tried to hurt Mary's chances of becoming

"Princess Clara" was a popular image on antique postcards. *Author's collection.*

engaged by sending a letter to William warning him of the insanity that was rampant in Ward's children.

Charles had the least amount of public drama, aside from his extravagant spending. He was not buried in the family plot in Elmwood Cemetery and possibly moved to Australia, according to genealogical records, but it cannot be said with certainty.

"Princess" Clara Ward

Eber's daughter Clara from his second marriage would take on a scandalous story of her own. Born on June 17, 1873, Clara grew up as an heiress and socialite. When she turned sixteen, she caught the eye of Joseph, Prince de Caraman-Chimay of Belgium, while in Europe. His princely title was more of a social classification than a political position. They were married shortly after they met, on May 19, 1890. He was

Clara Ward's "poses plastiques" on antique postcards. *Author's collection.*

almost twice her age at thirty-one years old and wasn't even considered to be the most handsome man, but Americans loved that one of their own had become a European princess, even if it was in title only.

Clara had two children with Joseph, but in November 1896, she met a charming and charismatic violinist, Rigó Jancsi, at a restaurant. One month later, she abandoned her husband and children and eloped with the "gypsy violinist." The prince divorced Clara, and she and Jancsi married. The story was outrageous, and gossip about "Princess Chimay's" escapades was published in both American and European newspapers.

Clara performed alongside Rigó in Europe and created her own performance art she called "poses plastiques," in which she donned a white bodysuit and posed in various ways that were considered risqué for the time. Images of her and Rigó made popular postcards, and even the French artist Henri de Toulouse-Lautrec created a lithograph of Clara and Rigó in 1897 called *Idylle Princière*. But their marriage would end a few years later, after he was unfaithful to her. Clara remarried twice more, but they were not as notorious as her first two marriages. She died in Padua, Italy, at the age of forty-three after an illness and left the rest of her inheritance to her two children.

A LEGACY FORGOTTEN

For someone who had such a major influence on the early development of the Midwest through lumber, steel, shipping and more, Eber's name is barely recognized today except by history buffs or fellow Michigan history enthusiasts. Eber's assets were quickly sold off, and his once powerful name vanished from everything he had built. The name "Catherine Ward" dominated the Ludington sawmills and warehouses as soon as she inherited the business. But she would later remarry and leave the Ward name behind. With no one in his family carrying on the Eber Brock Ward legacy, everything disappeared. As for Eber's reputation, the sensational reporting of newspapers characterized him as someone suffering from "insane delusions," and even the *New York Times* stated his life "is one of those narratives which would have been called monstrously improbable in fiction." The comfort he got from seeking the advice of mediums made the powerful businessman appear weak and gullible, and perhaps he was guilty of being just a touch impressionable in the presence of the spirits. Historian

Justin Wargo wrote, "The battle of Eber Brock Ward's will was one of the most significant American legal battles of the second half of the nineteenth century and was truly a case without parallel." Eber's vast empire did a lot to strengthen the Industrial Revolution, and Ward deserves a second chance to be remembered, even if we'd still rather read about the otherworldly and sensational details of his life than his ventures in mundane steel and lumber.

Part Two

LEGEND, LORE AND GHOSTS

6

THE LEGEND OF THE NAIN ROUGE

Large cities will always have ups and downs during their lifespans. Tragic accidents, fires, natural disasters and crime are all sad reminders that with the good sometimes comes the bad. But what if those bad things could easily be blamed on something other than humans or acts of God? What if they could be blamed on a small, red-faced dwarf-like creature with a set of pointed razor-sharp teeth? One of Detroit's oldest legends from the French settlers may very well provide such a scapegoat. The legendary creature is known as the Nain Rouge or the "Red Dwarf," and since Detroit's infancy, his appearance has been a sign of calamity and bad things to come that began with the founder of Detroit, Antoine Laumet de Lamothe Cadillac.

BEWARE!

On March 10, 1701, in St. Louis, Quebec, a party was held in honor of Cadillac. He had just been put in charge of the land that was destined to become the city of Detroit. As the party went into the night, a fortuneteller, complete with a black cat perched on her shoulder, came into the home and asked if she could offer her psychic services. She was welcomed in and was soon reading the palms of the influential and powerful people who were amazed by her supernatural ability. The mysterious woman approached

Cadillac, who allowed her to gaze into his palm. "Oh! I see you are going to start a great city!" she told him. Cadillac knew this to be true, so he urged her to continue, but the rest of her prophecy wasn't what any aspiring political man with ambitions wanted to hear. She told him that his new city would struggle under his rule and wouldn't become prosperous until another flag flew over the land.

Intrigued—maybe even worried—Cadillac pressed her for more information, wondering if he would leave an inheritance for his children. She warned him that it was entirely up to him to make better choices, but there was something else he needed to be cautious of besides his ego and blind ambition. "Beware of the Nain Rouge. Do not offend him. If you don't heed this warning, everything you work for along with your children's inheritance will vanish." She also cautioned him about selling liquor to the Native Americans, which the Jesuits strongly objected to. But Cadillac didn't like the Jesuits very much, and there was money to be made in selling to the tribes.

Not satisfied with his prediction, Cadillac scoffed at the woman and wrote her off as nothing more than petty entertainment. When he got home that night, he laughingly told his wife, Marie-Thérèse, what the fortuneteller had said to him. His wife went pale and warned him that she didn't think he should ignore what the fortuneteller said. The next day, Cadillac and a group of men sailed to "le detroit," or "the strait," to settle the new territory in the name of France.

Six years later, in May 1707, Cadillac and his wife were settled in Detroit and took an evening walk. Cadillac told his wife how "everything was coming together for him." As they passed by two men, the couple couldn't help but overhear them complaining about the current state of Detroit and their displeasure with it. Marie-Thérèse's body stiffened with panic, as she heard one of the men say that his wife saw "le petit Nain Rouge." The men's voices faded away as they walked on. Marie-Thérèse grabbed her husband's arm and said with worry in her voice, "It's the Nain Rouge the fortuneteller warned you about!"

Cadillac's arrogant laugh was abruptly cut short when, suddenly, a grotesque, small creature with reddish, ruddy skin and a sharp-toothed grin hobbled onto their path. Without delay, Cadillac thwacked the creature with his walking cane and yelled, "Get away!" The dwarf scurried off, releasing a maniacal laugh into the night air. He was warned to not offend the Nain Rouge if it ever crossed his path, but that's just what Cadillac did. Just like the fortuneteller had forewarned, Cadillac's luck took a turn for the worse, and everything she predicted about his doomed future came true for him. Was this because Cadillac disrespected the Nain Rouge all those years ago? Did this prove that he truly was a harbinger of doom and gloom, an entity that demanded respect or else?

MARIE HAMLIN, DETROIT'S EARLY FOLKLORIST

Marie Caroline Watson Hamlin was born on February 22, 1850, in Detroit and was an early folklorist, genealogist and historian. The story of the Nain Rouge was preserved in her book *Legends of Le Detroit*, first published in 1883. As a child, Marie listened to stories told by her elders and heard a combination of French and Native American tales. Stories of werewolves, phantom horses, prophecies, curses and, of course, the Nain Rouge were all part of the colorful local lore. Marie's love of local history also led her to conduct an extensive genealogy of Detroit's old French families, referencing

An illustration by Isabella Stewart of the Nain Rouge in *Legends of Le Detroit*. *Public domain.*

75

some of the city's earliest historical records and documents, along with records kept at Saint Anne's, Detroit's first and oldest Catholic church. In 1878, at age twenty-eight, she gave a speech to the Wayne County Pioneer Society about the French-Canadian heritage of Detroit. It can be assumed that there probably weren't a lot of women at that time giving lectures on their historical research and helping to preserve the stories of the culture they belonged to. Initially, Marie's legends were individually published in the *Detroit Free Press* from 1880 to 1881. Her column was so popular with Detroiters that she was asked to publish them in a book, which led to *Legends of Le Detroit*. The first print sold quickly, and a second edition was printed in 1884. The book was illustrated by Detroit native and artist Isabella Stewart.

A LIFE CUT SHORT

Marie's family was wealthy, and her ancestors established themselves in Detroit when it was nothing more than a trading post in the early eighteenth century. An early ancestor who died in 1796 left a large estate to the family in Springwells, just west of Detroit. Her father, John Watson, was also a successful merchant. Unfortunately, Marie suffered with tuberculosis for many years, often traveling to warmer climates during the winter for her health, but the disease took her life at the age of thirty-five. Her estate was valued around $27,000, a sum worth $756,000 today. In her will, she left a pearl necklace and earring set to Justine Joseph Moran of Detroit. Alice Hall, her goddaughter, received her diamond earrings. Many other friends and family members received between $50 and $100. Her largest gift was $1,000 to Saints Peter and Paul Jesuit Church, the oldest existing church building in Detroit (having laid its first cornerstone in 1844).

But the strangest clause in her will almost seemed inspired by one of the tricksters in the legends she wrote about. She stated that after her debts and gifts were paid, the rest of her estate was to go to her husband of seven years, William Yates Hamlin, but under one condition—if he were to ever remarry, he needed to give everything back to the family. One-half would then go to Marie's aunt Alexanderine L. Hall, and the rest was to be divided between orphanages and other charitable institutions. The clause became an issue when William was remarried on January 15, 1890, to Louise Helm, and with a vengeance, her family swooped in and filed suit to gain back what was left of the estate. But Judge Gartner was in favor of William and said that "the

The Nain Rouge is often depicted as impish or devil-like in appearance. *Painting by Amberrose Hammond.*

provision in restraint of marriage was void, that a provision of this nature was valid when applied to a woman, but invalid as to a man," and that the law did not uphold "postmortem jealousy."

James LaForest, on his blog, *The Red Cedar*, summed up Marie's legacy beautifully when he wrote: "In her work with French Canadian folklore, Hamlin became an activist for her culture and a figure in wider Detroit society, someone whose public works promoted integrity in understanding the many layers of Detroit's history. Without her work nearly 150 years ago, this dimension of folklore and tradition might have disappeared from our collective culture forever."

SIGHTINGS OF THE NAIN ROUGE

The following list contains the alleged moments the creature has been spotted before a calamity in Detroit's past.

- In May 1707, Cadillac was the first to encounter and smite the Nain Rouge, only to be removed from his office in 1710, much to his displeasure.

- On July 30, 1763, the dwarf was spotted near the Detroit River. The next day, Chief Pontiac killed over sixty men during the Battle of Bloody Run.
- Forty years later, in the spring of 1805, people saw the dwarf walking through the streets of Detroit. A couple of months later, on June 11, a horrible fire burned most of the town, and a lot of the city's early history and buildings were lost.
- General William Hull was the only officer in American history to be sentenced to death (but pardoned) for military incompetence after surrendering Fort Detroit to the British in 1813, even though the American side had far more men and could have fought back. He claimed he saw the dwarf before that event.
- During the Detroit riots in 1967, someone claimed to see the dwarf.
- On March 1, 1976, utility workers claimed they saw the dwarf climbing up a utility pole. Shortly after that, Detroit was hit with one of the worst ice storms the city had ever seen.
- An article in the *Daily Tribune* out of Royal Oak from October 1, 1986, mentioned the dwarf may have been seen hitching a ride on the Detroit People Mover. No horrible incident is connected with this joy ride.

MARCHE DU NAIN ROUGE

Unlike the other tales in *Legends of Le Detroit*, the story of the Nain Rouge has taken on a life of its own beyond Marie Hamlin's story. It has become one of the most celebrated legends in Detroit and even has a parade in its honor. The year 2009 marked the first Marche Du Nain Rouge, which was cofounded by Francis Grunow and Joe Uhl. The annual parade in midtown Detroit centers around the Nain

John E.L. Tenney and his pro-Nain signs for the Marche Du Nain Rouge. Visit www.weirdlectures.com. *Amberrose Hammond, photographer.*

Rouge legend. The event's original concept was to push the little imp out of the city once and for all and to bring luck and prosperity back to Detroit. The parade occurs every year around the spring equinox in March and has become a celebration of the strange and weird. There are decorated floats, brass bands and outlandish costumes. Many people dress up like the Nain Rouge, making themselves look slightly demonic or devil-like.

Michigan paranormal researcher John E.L. Tenney has long held a different theory about what the Nain Rouge really is—an ancient protector who warns Detroit citizens of impending disaster rather than cause it. Since the start of the parade, Tenney, with his punk-rock roots as a teenager growing up in Royal Oak, has protested the parade and brings signs that say, "Stop Nain Shame," "Nain Loves Detroit" and "B Nice 2 Nain." We don't want a parade disrespecting the creature if he's on our side, right? But Tenney says the "protest" is all in good fun, and overall, the parade is doing more to spread awareness of the old legend, whether he's a bad guy or a good guy in the end.

Cadillac. What a Jerk.

Antoine Laumet de Lamothe Cadillac was not the nicest of men, and perhaps he appeared in a legend about a little creature who brings misery because he himself was someone who brought misery to many people. He had a big ego and a desire to make a name for himself in the history books, no matter the cost. Cadillac's history is a shady one. It's been theorized that Cadillac lied about the rank and importance of his family, even creating a fake family crest and giving himself the title of "squire." He then convinced the powers that be in France to give him land grants in Novia Scotia and to allow him to further survey the land down the North American coast.

While stationed at Fort Michilimackinac, Cadillac's nastiness was on full display. He hated the Jesuit missionaries who had been there much longer than he had because, by their recommendation, the sale of alcohol to the local Native American tribes needed to be strictly limited. Cadillac didn't care about the restrictions and saw that there was money to be made by paying the Native Americans with rum rather than much-needed food and supplies in exchange for their fur pelts.

Once established at Fort Detroit, historian Mickey Lyons wrote, "Cadillac ran Detroit as a private fiefdom. He put French soldiers to work clearing

A romanticized illustration of Cadillac's life in the Detroit Public Library. *Courtesy of the Library of Congress.*

lands for settlement, then promptly charged them rent to set up houses on the land, all while refusing to supply their food from government funds." He was also known to throw people in jail simply because they didn't agree with him. His awfulness didn't go unnoticed, and Father Francois Vaillant, a Jesuit who had traveled with Cadillac to Detroit, sent complaints back to Montreal that documented his misdeeds. By September 1710, Cadillac, thanks to many other missteps and blunders, was finally asked to step down from his post at Detroit and go to the Louisiana Territories to become governor there. By 1717, Cadillac was asked to step down again, thanks to more poor decisions that led to severe monetary loss.

So, much like the Nain Rouge is said to be a creature who brings doom and gloom, perhaps its connection to Cadillac was born from the memories of those who remembered Cadillac to be an awful man who ruined many lives and knowingly caused pain and suffering among Native American tribes. Perhaps those memories were the origins of a legend about a man deservingly being "cursed" for his wickedness.

7

THE LONELY GHOST OF MINNIE QUAY

Forester was a small but thriving town on the shores of Lake Huron on the eastern side of the Thumb. In 1876, the logging business was booming. Ships came and went daily with lumber and other goods. Forester was a convenient port with long docks and four large warehouses, and the townsfolk were used to seeing sailors come and go, sometimes stopping for a break or to have a bite to eat at one of the inns. One of those sailors caught the eye of fifteen-year-old Mary Jane Quay, or "Minnie," as she was commonly called, and the young man noticed her, too. It can be imagined that she would wait by Smith's Dock, not far from her home, for his ship to arrive. He'd hop off the boat with a big, charming smile, and the two would take a walk before he had to leave again. Maybe his ship would sometimes stay the night, and the pair could spend more time together. But however they originally locked eyes, their time spent together began to generate malicious rumors and gossip, and with only about one thousand residents, it didn't take long for the news to spread through the town.

The rumors were of the worst kind for a young girl in a town where the tallest building was the Methodist church and saloons were prohibited. Rumors that she was ruined and possibly pregnant with the sailor's child found their way to her parents, James and Mary Ann, who were horrified and embarrassed. No parent wanted to see their daughter run off with a sailor, let alone be impregnated by one before marriage. After heated arguments, Minnie's parents forbid her from ever seeing him again. They didn't believe Minnie when she said the rumors about her weren't true. The *Sanilac Jeffersonian* wrote, "These stories have been bandied about the community with the usual recklessness of gossip and scandal and coming to the ears of her parents caused them to talk to the young girl in a manner that must have cut her to the heart."

Despondent and feeling shamed by an entire town, at 3:00 p.m. on Thursday, April 27, 1876, Minnie walked down to the docks and threw herself into the frigid early spring water of Lake Huron. Her brother, probably four-year-old James, saw her jump in and never come back to the surface. The little boy ran for help. Men ran to the docks, but it took them a full hour to retrieve her lifeless body. It was reported that Minnie left a suicide note that declared her innocence and chastised her parents for not believing her and for "being too severe." But even after her death, her parents still wanted proof that their daughter had been telling the truth. They asked Dr. Oldfield, the medical examiner, to do a full inspection of her body, "which failed to reveal any evidence of the truth of the stories

A 2007 photograph of Minnie Quay's family headstone at the Forester Township Cemetery. *Amberrose Hammond, photographer.*

concerning her." The gossip had indeed been false. James's and Mary Ann's hearts must have shattered for not believing their daughter. The *Sanilac Jeffersonian* further commented, "The sad event has cast a gloom over Forester, but doubtless, gossips and scandal mongers will look for some new victim." Minnie was buried in the Forester Township Cemetery, a victim of cruel gossip.

Her parents were probably distraught with guilt, wondering if they had chosen different words and not forbidden her from seeing him or had believed her from the start then they would still have a daughter, alive and well. Once the lumber business declined in the area, so, too, did the town of Forester. The area now exists mostly for campers and vacationers along Lake Huron.

MARIAN KUCLO AND THE GHOST OF MINNIE QUAY

Since Minnie's death, the memory of her tragedy has lived on through her ghost. Marian Kuclo wrote about the ghost story in her 1992 book, *Michigan Haunts and Hauntings*. Minnie's lonely and heartbroken ghost is said to sometimes be seen walking along the rocky shores of Lake Huron appearing as a white apparition, waiting for a ship to arrive with her sailor onboard. It became one of Marian's favorite stories after she heard it for the first time in 1980 while staying in a cottage along Lake Huron. Marian's version of the story contains a more romanticized version of Minnie's death, saying she flung herself into the water after learning her love's ship had sunk on the Great Lakes and that all onboard had drowned. Variations of legends are very common in folklore, and in addition to the apparition seen along the shore, Minnie's apparition has been said to try and lure other women into the water to join her. People have also reported hearing a girl sobbing but never being able to find the source.

Marian filed the story away and wrote an article for the *Detroit Free Press* seven years later, on October 4, 1987, that featured Michigan hauntings, including the Minnie Quay story, only Marian called her "Nellie Quay." Bill Clugston, the owner of the Forester Inn, one of the only old buildings still standing from the town's early days, reached out to Marian to politely correct a few errors in her article and invited her to come to Forester and learn more. Bill contacted her again in 1988 hoping Marian would be interested in hosting some ghost tours of the Thumb area via a charter bus. Even at $115 apiece, tickets sold fast. It was just the type of tourism people were hungry for. The ticket included "meals, a horse-drawn ride through the woods and visits to a variety of interesting and unusual old buildings between Detroit and Forester," with the tour finishing at the haunted Forester Inn with a candlelight séance at the Forester Township Cemetery conducted by Marian Kuclo, a practicing witch and known as the Green Witch Gundella.

THE MINNIE QUAY PROTEST

In Bad Axe, just north of Forester, the Faith Gospel Tabernacle Church heard about the tours that would include a séance given by a self-proclaimed "witch." Reverend James Willett and his forty church members got so worked up over the idea that they decided to protest the Sunday, June 19, 1988, tour of thirty-two people. The church members circled Minnie's tombstone to block Marian from getting anywhere near it. Two days later, when Marian came through with another tour, the church members had brought giant eight-foot crosses that read "Jesus Loves U" on them. Holding their crosses high, the church members walked down the middle of Highway 25 in front of the cemetery. Bill Clugston remembered that locals were so intrigued by the event that they set chairs up on the side of the road and just watched the spectacle take place.

Tour members were a little taken aback by the protests and didn't think the extra drama was necessary, many of them saying it was just for fun and that they didn't really believe in ghosts or think what they were doing was evil. But Reverend Willett told the *Detroit Free Press*, "We feel that witchery, sorcery and communicating with the spirits of the dead is an abomination of God. We feel we have a responsibility to take a stance against this form of evil." The reverend believed they "drove evil spirits out of Forester that day." But Marian cleverly responded, "He is never going to get rid of the ghosts of Forester. The people are going to keep them alive for years," which is exactly what has happened as Forester has become synonymous with the ghost and legend of Minnie Quay.

For the rest of her life, Marian would become used to people misunderstanding her. She was born in Port Huron in 1930 and grew up in a family who practiced a witchcraft tradition that went back to their Scottish roots. It was a form of early European paganism that had nothing to do with the devil, demons or anything evil. It revered nature, and spells were a way to simply focus one's intention on a positive, desired outcome; it was not something used as a weapon or to curse. She told the *Michigan Daily*, "Witches believe not in the devil, but in their own power." She also firmly believed in the power of positive thinking.

Highly educated, Marian went to Central Michigan University, Eastern University and Wayne State University, earning a bachelor's and a master's degree in education. She taught elementary school for over two decades and was well loved around southeast Michigan. She was a theatrical person and would often appear in public with her trademark large spider pendant necklace that looked like it contained secret powers of its own. She was known for her storytelling; her witchy advice columns, "Witch Watch," "Kitchen Witch" and "Witch Words," which were published in newspapers in the metro Detroit area from the mid-1970s through the early 1990s; and her "love potions." Out of all the services she provided as a witch, from tarot to astrological readings, Marian said love potions were her number one request.

THANK THE LUMBERJACKS

Minnie's tragedy made an impression on people long before they started to see her ghost, and it was Michigan's lumberjacks who preserved and passed on her story through their ballads. If it wasn't for the lumberjacks, Minnie's story would have just been confined to a few articles in century-old newspapers. Earl Clifton Beck, an English professor at Central Michigan University, gathered lumberjack ballads from all over the state and saved a version of Minnie Quay's ballad in his *Songs of the Michigan Lumberjacks*, published in 1941 and revised and updated in 1948 as *Lore of the Lumber Camps*. Beck called "Minnie Quay" a "bunkhouse ballad," which he described as a song that made "no mention of lumbermen or lumber woods." Songs like these were sung after dinner and before the early lumberjack bedtime of 9:00 p.m. as a form of entertainment. Beck stated that Owen Noffsinger of Saganing, Michigan, "said some singers called the song 'Winnie Gray' and that it was first sung by William J. Smith of Port Huron." The following is a version of the ballad that was sung by a Mrs. William Barnes of Port Sanilac sometime before 1941.

"The Ballad of Minnie Quay"

'Twas in the town of Forester,
Along the sandy shore,
The voice of one poor Minnie Quay
We'll never hear no more.

Her soul is sweetly resting
For the Judgment Day to come,
When all shall render up accounts
And the Judge pronounce our doom.

This fair maid was only sixteen,
She was scarcely in her bloom,
When her parents they got angry
And wished her in her tomb.

They said they wished that she was dead,
For some young man one day
Went and told an untruthful story
About poor Minnie Quay.

One day her parents went away
And left her all alone,
Alone with her little brother,
Until they should return.

Little did they think when they'd return
They'd find their daughter dead,
Gone to a land that is far fairer,
Where no more tears are shed.

'Twas on the twenty-sixth of April
Her parents went away.
Down by the side of Lake Huron
This fair one she did stray.

A-pondering on the dreadful scene
Which quickly must pass by,

For she had now determined
In a watery grave to lie.

She waved her hand to Forester
As if to say good-by;
Then quickly in Lake Huron
Her body it did lie.

Before anyone could render help,
Could lend a helping hand,
Her spirit it was borne away
Unto the Promised Land.

Now sweetly she is resting
In a cold and silent grave.
If her parents had not condemned her,
This fair one might have been saved.

But again her friends will meet her
If by the Savior they are led
To a land that is far better,
Where no farewell tears are shed.

THE IMMORTAL MINNIE QUAY

At over 145 years old, it's clear that Minnie Quay will continue to live on through the folklore her story has created. Marian stated the ballad printed in her book *Michigan Haunts and Hauntings* was her "favorite version," but it's very probable that Marian waved her creative wand over her version and tweaked it a bit with her flair for storytelling. Based on historical records, it does not appear that the real reason Minnie killed herself was because of her love's boat sinking but more because of the shame and humiliation her town and family cast over her. Marian continued to research her favorite ghost story and wrote that she came "across additional information that leads me to believe that perhaps she did not take her own life after all" and that she was "writing a book about the ghost of Minnie Quay." But sadly, Marian lost her life to cancer in 1993.

Minnie's "legend" has become a permanent fixture of Michigan's ghost lore and continues to attract paranormal enthusiasts to the shores of Lake Huron in search of her ghost. Some even claim that the old home across from the Forester Inn was where Minnie lived and is haunted, but in the 1962 book *Thumb Diggins* by Neva DuMond, it was written that the home actually belonged to Minnie's younger brother Charles, who died in 1966. Over the years, Minnie's pink granite tombstone in the Forester Township Cemetery has been showered with coins, trinkets and flowers. The original tombstones are long gone. Coins are commonly left on the headstone and have different meanings from just being a token of remembrance to being a charm left behind so her "ghost" doesn't follow them home. Her story will continue to endure, and if her spirit is forever wandering in search of her love, may she find some much-needed peace someday or at least relish in the fact that she is remembered and not forgotten.

8

HAUNTED ROADS AND MYSTERIOUS LIGHTS

Two legends of ghostly roads that have been popular in Michigan for decades are those of Detroit's Knock-Knock Street and Denton Road in Canton. From making a deal with the devil at the crossroads to famous hitchhiking ghosts, like Chicago's Resurrection Mary, legends surrounding roads have been around the world for centuries. Jan Harold Brunvand wrote, "The legends we tell, as with any folklore, reflect many of the hopes, fears and anxieties of our time." Roads get us to where we need to go, but they can also present a constant threat to our lives, especially with the invention of the automobile. Deadly crashes leave behind the memory of a life taken too soon that leaves a ghost story in its wake. Or while driving, a mysterious light or object is seen by motorists, and a story builds around it to offer some type of earthly or otherworldly explanation. Sometimes, a mysterious story even surrounds a perfectly mundane situation—such is the case with Knock-Knock Street—but mundane or not, nothing gets in the way of a good story.

THE LEGEND OF KNOCK-KNOCK STREET

A driver, alone in their car late at night, slows down for a stop sign. It's a warm summer night, and the sound of crickets is the only thing that can be heard. Looking left and right, the driver is startled by the sight of a little girl standing on the sidewalk under a streetlamp. She looks pale under the artificial light and out of place. Not another human is in sight. "Is this girl alone? Is she lost?" the driver wonders, but something doesn't feel natural. A sound startles the driver, and they look away from the girl for a moment, only to look back and find her staring into their driver's side window. Her eyes are vacant and hollow looking. She knocks on the window and asks, "Are you the driver who killed me?"

The preceding story is a retelling of Detroit's Knock-Knock Street legend. Similar versions have circulated by word of mouth and, years later, on the Internet, but the story dates to the 1950s. Folklorist Richard Dorson first wrote about the legend in his book *American Folklore*, published in 1959. Dorson wrote that different streets have been pegged as "the street" over the years, but all of the stories agree that "a little girl was struck and killed by a hit-and-run driver and that ever since, cars driving over that street hear bumps from the child's body dragging behind the fender." More gruesome accounts exist that say "one of her arms was cut off" and that the arm is thumping against the doors of passing cars. Even rumors of a curse placed on the road by the poor girl's parents were put in the mix. Another story says she was riding her bike when she was hit by a car and desperately knocked on the car to get the driver's attention, but the driver never heard her and still ran her over. Another version of the legend shared with this author came from a woman who grew up with the Knock-Knock Street tales. She remembered it being told to her as a "cautionary tale":

> *A girl who turned sixteen received a beautiful convertible for her birthday and planned to take her friends for a joy ride in it. The girl's little sister wanted badly to go with, but she was told she couldn't because she was "too young" to hang out with them. The girl picked her friends up, and they rode around, having fun, until they drove through a stoplight and caused an accident. As the girls got out of the car, they heard thumping coming from the trunk of the car. Cautiously approaching the trunk, they opened it to find the girl's badly injured little sister who had hidden in the trunk in a desperate attempt to hang with the "older girls." She passed away from her injuries. The moral of the story was to "let your little siblings hang out with you," lest something bad should happen to them.*

The actual street that caused the original commotion was Strasburg Street on Detroit's east side. The legend gained so much attention that a police officer had to be stationed on the road to monitor the throngs of curious, thrill-seeking drivers looking for the ghost or hoping to hear the sounds for themselves. No actual event exists to uphold the story of a little girl dragged to her death in a hit-and-run accident, but upon investigation, a reason why people were hearing the strange knockings was discovered. The *Detroit Free Press* wrote on July 16, 1961, that it had been ten years since the Strasburg Street story first surfaced and that "when the teenagers drove their cars over the street, sure enough, there came an eerie *rap, rap, rap*. The girls squealed. The boys protected them with a comforting arm."

The city investigated the source of the sounds and "found that after the heat of the day, the concrete slabs contracted and wobbled. The edges grated, and thumping echoed in cars." In 1952, the road was repaired and resurfaced to send the "ghost" into the light. Richard Dorson mentioned that other streets had been branded "Knock-Knock Street," and in 1967, Robert John Street in Saint Clair Shores earned the nickname, and people told the same story that the ghost of a girl who was killed would bang on your car. It appears the same situation with the pavement contracting was happening there as well.

The Mysterious Lights of Denton Road

Reports of eerie lights appearing around Denton Road in Canton and specifically what was once an old, single-lane wooden bridge over the Lower River Rouge have excited thrill-seekers since the 1960s. Supernatural folklore surrounding bridges often has a tragic backstory that took place on an ambiguous date in the past, and the Denton Road story is no different, with its own tragic legend that explains the origins of the lights seen and the apparition of the "Blue Lady."

The Legend of the Blue Lady

Long ago, near the old Denton Road bridge, a husband and wife with a new baby lived in a farmhouse. All seemed fine in the husband's world until he discovered his wife in the arms of another man. Blind with rage, he grabbed an axe and swung, murdering the man in one bloody chop. Horrified, his wife grabbed their baby and ran from the house as fast as she could, hiding for her life under the Denton Road bridge, but her husband found her and killed her. No one ever knew what became of the husband or the baby, but it's been said that an eerie blue apparition has been seen in the area that is the ghost of the mother, forever searching for her baby. Another account says the light seen represents the lantern the woman held as she ran for safety.

This piece of folklore gives an otherworldly explanation for the reports of strange lights that have been seen through the decades, but humans—very much alive—can be blamed for creating some of the eerie lights people have witnessed. Virginia Bailey Parker collected a few memories of the lights from locals for the Canton Historical Society in her 1998 book *Ghost Stories and Other Tales from Canton*, and some of the biggest culprits behind the lights were college students from nearby Eastern Michigan University.

Parker wrote that Canton resident Terry Bennett remembered fraternity pledges being dropped off in the middle of wooded farmland along Denton Road and supplied with only a lantern to find their way back to the school in the middle of the night. The lantern lights of the students were seen by the occasional driver at night, and that person would excitedly tell someone about the "mysterious lights" or the "Blue Lady" apparition they saw. But in fact, it was nothing more than a college freshman wondering about their life choices at that moment. Dorothy West was a lifelong resident of Canton and admitted that her sixteen-year-old son, Dan, and his friend Johnny would drive up and down the road with a lantern on a fishing pole hanging out of the car window around the late 1950s to early 1960s.

In the past, people would also park near the bridge, turn off their car and wait for the "spook lights" to appear (which, for all they knew, was a lost fraternity pledge). Many were disappointed when they didn't see anything, but a few claimed they did indeed witness phantom lights come out of nowhere. Some reports have even claimed they were "chased" by the lights, giving them the name the "Denton Demon." So, was there possibly something mysterious going on that started the stories in the first place? Were some of the lights and experiences genuine anomalies that couldn't be blamed on a fraternity or kids hiding under the bridge waiting to prank unsuspecting motorists?

A woman shared her experience on Denton Road with this author and said that sometime in the 1960s, she saw three white lights, somewhat large, glowing in the sky and moving over a cornfield toward her and her friends. The witness and her friends continued to drive down the road, watching the lights move in the sky. As the lights moved closer and hovered over their car, the engine cut out. Everyone in the car panicked, thinking that the "ghost" of Denton Road was upon them. They started the car back up and got out of there as fast as they could. Electrical malfunctions have long been a sign of something ghostly as well as something extraterrestrial. Other people all over the United States with similar stories have had their cars stall after a strange light in the sky hovered over their vehicle. Some of them have even reported missing time after the event, finding it to be hours later than they remember after their car starts back up.

Denton Road wasn't the only area of southeast Michigan that was experiencing strange lights in the sky in the 1960s. Eighty-four miles away from Denton Road is the town of Hillsdale, which became a UFO (unidentified flying object) hotspot in 1966 because of a mass sighting of bizarre lights traveling in the sky known as the "Swamp Gas" case. Trustworthy and honest people witnessed the strange display—police officers, firefighters and everyday average people—on March 20, 1966. The sightings were ultimately dismissed and blamed on swamp gas from nearby marshlands by Dr. J. Allen Hynek, who was working for the United States government program Project Bluebook. The program's purpose was to collect UFO reports and data. Even future president Gerald R. Ford, then a senator, demanded that the people who witnessed the lights get a better explanation than swamp gas, which no one believed. Were some of the strange lights people witnessed at Denton Road and blamed on ghosts possibly something not even of this planet? Southeast Michigan in the 1960s was definitely having a moment of high strangeness.

Construction in 2003 modernized the old Denton Road bridge, and it's now not the old, creepy, graffiti-covered relic it once was. Nevertheless, reports of strange, eerie blue orbs of light and other paranormal happenings by the bridge persist, and paranormal enthusiasts still drive down the road hoping to see something strange. The area is now residential, so any person who hopes to observe the strange phenomenon needs to be respectful to the residents. But maybe the lights are still out there, waiting to show up to drivers in the middle of the night at the most unexpected moment. Let's just hope the lights don't get in the habit of abducting any of the curiosity seekers.

9

THE JACKSON DISTURBANCE

Victor Lincoln picked up his shotgun and walked toward the basement door. His family had just heard heavy footsteps walking up the stairs and then a sudden pounding on his son's bedroom door, which sent the fifteen-year-old Thomas running from his room in a panic. Victor opened the door, expecting to come face to face with an intruder, but no one was there. He looked all around the basement and the rest of the home but couldn't find any reason for the loud sounds the family had heard. Their dog whined and seemed nervous, as if it, too, sensed something was off. Whatever had made the noises had announced its arrival that night, on October 30, 1961, just in time for Halloween, and it planned on sticking around for a while.

The Lincoln home in Jackson, Michigan, had been in the Lincoln family for fifty years, and the house was said to be quite old, possibly built in the 1830s and added onto over the years, but for the past couple of years, the family had been noticing strange things. Sometimes, when they left, they would come back to find the house in disarray, with objects knocked over or a faucet running. This initially led them to believe someone was breaking into their home. The police were called to come look the house over, but other than someone playing pranks on them, there was no other logical explanation for the things going on in their home while they were gone. After October 30, that all changed when whatever was moving objects in their home no longer required them to be gone.

For the next couple of months, unpredictable and disturbing things that made absolutely no sense took place consistently. On windless days, cold wind would be felt moving through the home. Glasses and dishes flew from the shelves on their own and smashed to pieces on the floor. Water faucets turned on by themselves. Cupboard doors opened and closed. Beds that were made would be unmade hours later. A book was once found on a bed eerily opened to a page about the afterlife. The TV and phone would act up, and the sound of someone snoring was sometimes heard coming from one of the bedrooms when it was unoccupied. Lamps fell, and books would appear in stacks of ten or more around the house. At Christmastime, the lights and tinsel were pulled from the tree while the family was sitting around it in their living room. They took the tree down immediately, knowing it would just happen again. Sometimes, the activity became dangerous, such as the gas stove turning on by itself and a small paring knife that flew from a drawer and hit Beatrice Lincoln in her leg, leaving a small cut. Even more bizarre was a large steel cabinet that fell over on its own without making a sound, as if it fell over somewhere in its own space and time.

News about the "haunted house" in Jackson spread, and reporters eager to interview the family living with a rowdy ghost were surprised to find a shaken but very normal household. Victor didn't shy away from telling reporters that what his family was experiencing wasn't a figment of their imagination. "It's as true as I'm standing here," he stated. Their twenty-two-year-old son, John, was living at home after being discharged from the army in August 1961. He was so frustrated by the activity that he told reporters, "I got so mad, I started swearing at our ghost. I used some pretty profane stuff. Then, a plastic bottle sailed off a kitchen cabinet, around the kitchen door and broke a window in the dining room. I guess it got mad at me, too." Harry Kellar, a local police officer, visited the family after he heard about the strange happenings. He wanted to see the activity for himself, though he was skeptical.

During his visit with the Lincolns, a bathroom faucet turned on by itself and the gas stove burners turned on, but no one had been cooking. Kellar was dumbfounded.

William G. Roll and the Psychical Research Foundation

Beatrice Lincoln was highly insulted when "a minister—I won't mention his name—stood up in church and told the congregation that the devil was in our house and had something to do with our family. I call that pretty narrow-minded," she told a reporter. After ignorant comments like that, clearly, the Lincolns were not interested in the clergy being pulled into the matter. Wanting to find someone who could give the family answers without harsh judgment, Victor's son-in-law Edward Eden sent a letter to Professor J.B. Rhine of Duke University in Durham, North Carolina. Joseph Banks Rhine, along with psychologist William McDougall, cofounded and opened the Parapsychology Laboratory in 1930 at Duke, where, for the first time, the empirical study of paranormal phenomena was being taken seriously in a university setting. The letter, still in existence in William Roll's archives at the University of West Georgia, verifies that the family was indeed dealing with something troubling that they had no explanation for. "I've never believed in ghosts, but something is going on here that we don't understand," Victor Lincoln told the media.

In 1962, Dr. William G. Roll was the research director of the Psychical Research Foundation, an offshoot of the Duke University laboratory, when details of the Lincoln family were brought to his attention. Roll took an active interest in the case and made the trip from North Carolina to Michigan to investigate, hoping to observe the phenomena in real time.

The type of activity the Lincoln family was dealing with was known as RSPK, or recurrent spontaneous psychokinesis, more commonly known as "poltergeist activity." *Poltergeist* is German for "noisy ghost," and its signature trait is the sudden movement of objects, often in a violent manner. William Roll coined the term *RSPK* and would go on to become one of the world's leading researchers in poltergeist phenomena during his lifelong position as the research director of the Psychical Research Foundation and later as a professor at the University of West Georgia until his death at the age of eighty-five on January 9, 2012.

Roll spent four days at the Lincolns' home in December 1961 and came back during the last week of January 1962. He interviewed the family and meticulously documented and observed everything, creating detailed diagrams of the home. When asked, he declined to comment on his thoughts and findings to local newspapers until a finished report was drawn up. Nothing about the home's past led anyone to believe in the usual tales

December 5, 1961
6019 So. Jackson Rd.
R#1
Jackson, Michigan

re: My Phone Call to
Professor Zener on
December 4, 1961.

Professor J. B. Rhine
Duke University
Durham, North Carolina

Dear Sir:

On the day of November 28, there were strange oc-
currences at the home of my father-in-law.

At 2:30 A.M. on November 30, they left their home,
and upon arriving at my home, they reported that the house in
which they lived was haunted. They reported instances of
bedding turning back by itself, as well as others.

On Friday, December 1, my father-in-law, four outsiders
~~members of the family~~, and myself went to this house. During
the time we were present, bedding turned back when no one was
in the bedrooms.

Many incidents have occurred at that residence since
December 1, and I have a detailed list of dates, approximate
time of day, those present in the house, etc.

I understand that you people are interested in this
type of matter, and we would appreciate it if you would
contact us to see if this situation can be rectified.

Yours very truly,

Edward J. Eden

EJE/mm

Edward J. Eden
6019 So. Jackson Rd.
R#1
Jackson, Michigan
Phone: STate-4-9643

Above: An original family letter sent to Duke University in search of help. *From the University of West Georgia, Ingram Library, Special Collections.*

Opposite: An original drawing of the Lincoln home by William Roll, which was made during his research trips. *From the University of West Georgia, Ingram Library, Special Collections.*

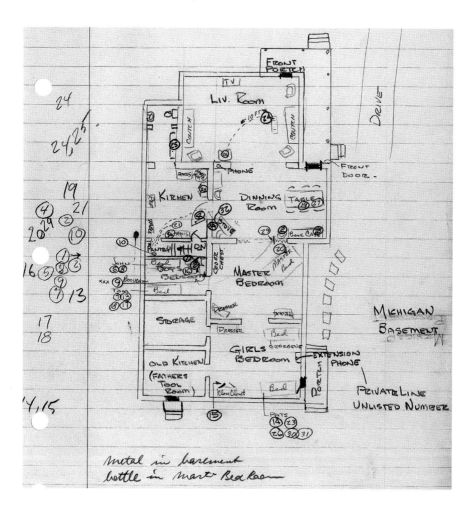

of terror that create a good ghost story, apart from it being old. Victor said the home was built over an old mine shaft, where prisoners from the nearby Michigan State Prison were put to work, but the mining wasn't prosperous, and the shaft was closed. William Roll theorized that part of the phenomena in the Lincoln home seemed to be linked to a deceased family member. Victor described the house as being "sick," and maybe it was. The strange activity escalated after the house was put up for sale. The home had been in the family since 1912, and the Lincolns joked that a past relative wasn't too happy with them leaving.

A Family Tragedy Discovered

Ghosts are often the result of a tragic event and are left behind after a life is taken unexpectedly or too soon. A glimpse into the Lincoln family's past showed the biggest human tragedy of them all—murder.

Victor's father, John Lincoln, was killed during a holdup by a teenage bandit named Emery Lapp on the evening of February 27, 1918, at 11:00 p.m. John and his friend Herman Wetzell were walking home from bowling when Emery stepped out of the shadows and confronted the men for money. John resisted and attempted to fight off the bandit, but armed with a loaded pistol, Emery fired, and a bullet lodged itself in John's heart. Emery ran, but police were able to find and arrest him the following day. He confessed to the killing and a few other past holdups. He was charged with first-degree murder. A year later, on December 26, 1919, Emery beat up a prison guard to escape from jail, which affected his chances of parole, but in 1936, Governor Frank Murphy reduced his sentence to forty years. At the time of John's murder, his wife, Eva, was pregnant with their daughter, Luella, who was born a couple of months later in May. Victor Lincoln was just a few months shy of two years old at the time. With a new baby and a toddler, Eva's parents, John and Melvina Warrington, moved into the Jackson home to help raise the family.

The Lincolns would experience the phantom smell of bread baking when none was being made and the sound of organ music playing the song "Rock of Ages" and sometimes even bagpipe music. Victor's grandmother held many prayer meetings at the home, during which an organ was played, and she always baked fresh bread. William Roll would not go on to formally publish anything about what he called the "Jackson Disturbance" in his personal files, but the public still wanted to know what he had concluded. Reporter Marjorie Eicher followed up with Roll while he was at the Parapsychological Association Convention in New York in September 1963.

In a *Detroit Free Press* article from October 10, 1963, she reported that the "Jackson Case" became one of thirty-two known cases of apparent recurrent spontaneous psychokinesis phenomena to be studied by scientists. Because of the quick response on the part of the Lincolns, "it is one of few alleged poltergeist cases to be observed scientifically while the phenomena were still taking place." Roll stated that "in poltergeist cases, there are usually two parties concerned—the one against whom phenomena is directed and the agent." The agent is the person (often a teenager) unconsciously causing the activity by using psychokinesis (PK), a parapsychological term that describes the ability to move things with the mind. In the case of the Lincolns, Roll felt no one in the family was an "agent," even though two teenage children were living at home. Roll mentioned the strange behavior of the family dog and said it was always "keeping watch in the hall, controlling access to the boy's bedroom." On one occasion, Roll said they noticed the dog become "restless" and run to the boy's bedroom door. When they opened the door, no one was inside, but the bedsheets had been turned down. Roll remade the bed and checked the windows. They were shut, and there were no footprints beneath the window in the fresh snow outside. It didn't take long before they discovered the bedsheets turned down again.

Roll also said the Jackson case was "one of five scientifically noted cases in which there were physical events for which there was no known reasonable explanation and in which the phenomena were related to deceased persons." Roll believed the case had more to do with a traditional haunting than an actual poltergeist case, which is why he never included it in any of his future writings on poltergeist studies, but the case was still unique to him. So, were the Lincolns being haunted by a past family member?

In 1963, William Roll said the Psychical Research Foundation considered the case still under study, but the Lincoln family had had enough and finally moved during the summer of 1962. Future homeowners Clyde Beauchamp and his wife didn't experience anything unusual in the home. Mrs. Beauchamp said she loved living in the home and wouldn't move, "even if the ghosts came back." Many years later, when asked to comment on the haunting for a Halloween-themed article in the *Detroit Free Press* on October 26, 1980, Thomas Lincoln, then in his thirties, declined to comment and said, "I don't want to drag it up. It isn't too pleasant." The family never tried to capitalize on their story beyond what they told newspaper reporters. In the end, William Roll seemed to believe the home was just haunted, rather than actual true poltergeist activity caused by one of their children. When the family moved away from the old home, hopefully, their ghostly troubles moved on, too.

Part Three

THE STRANGE AND UNUSUAL

10

"YE SHALL SEE STRANGE VISIONS"

Scattered throughout Michigan's past are little moments in which people thought they were genuinely being afflicted by old-fashioned witchcraft—the wart on the nose, old lady brewing an evil potion over a cauldron, "double, double, toil and trouble" kind of witches and witchcraft—a far cry from the gentle, nature-based religion of modern-day witchcraft practitioners. They could make you sick, kill your livestock or curse your whole family. Many of the superstitions were remnants of the old world that came over with people when they immigrated to the United States. The following stories are a few of these instances from Michigan's past.

"You all ought to be spanked for such superstition," was the exclamation of Judge Lemkie to the courtroom in the Wayne County Courthouse in Detroit on April 10, 1910. Mrs. Skowerinski was in trouble for punching Josephine Gawronski. Mrs. Skowerinski hadn't felt well, so she visited a local "witch doctor," who told her that her stomach problems were the result of being "bewitched." Both women had recently been to a wedding where Josephine had given Mrs. Skowerinski a drink. Mrs. Skowerinski came to believe that was the moment she had been cursed, so she found Josephine and punched her, hoping the punch would reverse the curse. Her stomach problems persisted, and the judge ordered her to pay Josephine twenty-five dollars in damages.

The people of Graafschap, a small village of Dutch immigrants next to Holland, Michigan, had a witchcraft scare around 1889. A sickness went around and passed through the village, most likely a cold or flu virus, but old superstitions die hard, and villagers wondered if they were bewitched. Anyone who was sick was encouraged to rip open their pillows and inspect the down feathers. If some of the clumps of feathers resembled a crow or chicken, that was a sure sign that they were bewitched. Seven crows and two chickens were found, and these "feather devils" needed to be burned immediately. A woman's butter wouldn't churn no matter how hard she worked at it, so with everything else going on in the village, she figured she was bewitched, too. So, her husband threw a red-hot poker into the butter, and the problem was solved. It was believed the hot metal purged the evil from the butter, and his wife was able to churn it.

Another Graafschap man did the pillow test and found the shapes of crows. Terrified and already in poor health, he determined that sleeping in his barn in a wagon was a better alternative to sleeping inside his cursed home. A doctor was called in to check on him, and a proper treatment was administered that had nothing to do with curse removal that quickly improved his health. The local minister saw the hysteria building and addressed the subject in a sermon he titled "Ye Shall See Strange Visions," which he delivered to a packed congregation hoping their minister had a plan to battle the evil that had befallen the village. Whatever the contents of the sermon were, it cooled the fires in their superstitious minds, and life returned to normal again.

On January 25, 1917, in Detroit, on Twenty-Eighth and Buchanan Streets, rumors that a girl had "turned herself into a lion, a bear or a devil" were being whispered in the neighborhood. Celia Wrobleski was sixteen years old and worked in a cigar factory in Detroit. She was a normal teenager and was described as having an "ordinary appearance," but wild rumors that she could turn herself into a variety of animals had settled into the illogical parts of citizens' brains. *The Detroit News* wrote, "The whisper of witchcraft turned back the clock of enlightened civilization in a day."

As the rumors spread, people started to gather in front of the poor girl's house. The first evening, police had to scatter two hundred people gawking and waiting. The second night, it was reported at least one thousand people had gathered. One neighbor said she could turn into a lion; another one said she could shapeshift into a lion and a bear. "No two stories agree as to the evil spirit which is said to possess the girl," the *Detroit Free Press* wrote, and people were even calling her a "devil child." Frustrated beyond belief, Celia told her friends, "Look at me. I'm just like you. I'm a girl. I'm not a devil or a bear or a lion." But even her friends looked at her with doubt. One piece of gossip floating around was that Celia, a Catholic, "was engaged to a Protestant.

An old engraving of a witch casting spells in her cauldron. *Public domain.*

She took the communion offerings from the church to divide with him and then cut the host into four pieces, and the wafers started to bleed. The man to whom she was engaged disappeared, and she became a lion." Another version said that when she turned into a lion, she attacked the man and sent him to the hospital, and yet another wild story said she turned him into stone. When questioned about this particular story, Celia was just confused, stating, "I am not engaged," and "I have never had a beau." Her church had to get involved to "combat the wave of superstition." Her priest, Father Bernard Jarzembowski, showed up to face the crowd and sternly lectured the lot, telling them they should all be ashamed of themselves. And during his sermon the following Sunday at Saint Francis's Church, he "denounced the rumors from his pulpit." Celia's parents blamed "spiteful relatives" for starting the strange rumors.

11

DRIVEN MAD BY WITCHCRAFT

Sarah Sumner's young child had died. How the child died is not known, but illness and disease were the likely culprits. Sarah still had a young infant to care for, but she fell into a deep depression and could barely function. Concerned for her daughter and grandchild, her mother, Sarah Whitney, told her to come live with her, which may not have been the best solution for her depression. The small house on farmland in Mount Morris Township measured only sixteen by twenty feet and consisted of a pantry, two bedrooms and another room that served every other purpose.

During the night, the family started to hear strange and unusual sounds outside the tiny home. They claimed to hear a lamb bleating and a horse whinney, animals they did not own. Stranger yet was the sound of a mockingbird singing and a bizarre buzzing sound, as if a swarm of bees were hovering over the home; and, even more disturbing, they claimed they would hear someone yelling the word *murder* and could smell burning flesh in the air. They became convinced they had become the victims of witches.

Dr. Luman L. Fuller from nearby Clio had been tending to Sarah Sumner. He knew her mental state was fragile after the death of her child, and it was causing her physical health to decline fast. On July 30, 1884, Dr. Fuller decided to go check on her, and as he knocked on the door of the home, he heard someone yell, "Go away!" Before he could react, the door swung open, and Sarah's sister Rosina lunged at the doctor with a pocketknife and left a small slash in his chest. After the attack, the police had no other choice but to get involved. The family had been acting strangely for weeks and were the topic of many stories around Mount Morris. The sound of gunfire coming from their property day and night had also been a daily and annoying occurrence for neighbors.

When the police arrived on the property, they were not quite prepared for the bedlam they uncovered. An article from the *Detroit Free Press* wrote, "The filth and squalor cannot be described." Police found Sarah Sumner naked and laying on a dirty bed, clutching her little baby tightly to her chest. She looked as if she were made of just skin and bones. But it wasn't just Sarah, her sister and her mother living in the tiny home; there was a total of sixteen people from adults to young children dressed in nothing but rags. Police learned the family believed themselves to be bewitched and put the blame on Adelbert Sumner, Sarah's husband. They claimed he was a witch after he showed an interest in or suggested Spiritualism and mediumship to the family. Clearly opposed to Spiritualism, Sarah Sumner and her family believed Adelbert had somehow caused the death of the child. They boldly asked the police to kill Adelbert to make everything stop. Adelbert was described as "a man of less than ordinary ability, but is a harmless, inoffensive individual who seems to have had sense enough about him to keep clear of the universal hallucination that has attacked the rest of the family."

Accessing the rest of the situation, the glass of the home's four windows had been smashed out, and the windows were covered with blankets. It was the middle of summer and hot outside, but a large cast-iron stove in the middle of the home was stuffed with wood and belching thick waves of heat into the house. The home smelled putrid and vile. The covered windows and extreme heat's purpose was to keep witches from entering. Fires had also been lit around the exterior perimeter, creating a fiery border of protection. The constant gunfire heard by neighbors had been the family shooting bits of silver into the air, further hoping to keep the witches away. Silver has long been associated with warding off evil.

Even more shocking was that the family believed the few farm animals they owned had become cursed by witches, so they cut off a portion of the cows' and pigs' tails to break the spell. They even took a small slice of the family dog's ear. And it wasn't just the animals they mutilated. One report from the *Detroit Free Press* on August 2, 1884, stated they had "cut off the tips of a number of their own fingers and toes…to relieve the stagnation of the blood in their veins and allow it to flow more freely." Blood from their animals was used to draw marks on their chests as sigils to ward off evil.

After the story was revealed in the newspapers, people felt sorry for the family. It was clear they were living in extreme poverty and suffering

An old medieval woodcut of a classic witch and her toad familiars. *Public domain.*

from mental illness. Sarah Whitney had had somewhere around fourteen children—no easy number to care for, especially after her husband, Robert, passed away in 1878.

Sarah Whitney, her daughters Sarah and Rosina and the rest of the family were picked up by a police wagon and brought to the Flint jail on the charge of disturbing the peace. While in jail, the women had a lot of curious visitors and gladly spoke with everyone who came by. A judge decided there was no point in formally charging the family because they were "insane" and needed to be medically evaluated. It was decided that Sarah Whitney and her children and grandchildren would be sent to the county poor farm. County poor farms were places where the elderly, crippled, mentally ill and poor could live and sometimes work if they had nowhere else to go or no one else to care for them. Doctors evaluated Sarah Sumner and Rosina and suggested they spend some time in the Pontiac Asylum.

12

FRANK LESNER, WITCH KILLER

Frank Lesner seemed stressed, and his supervisor felt that maybe a little time away from the job would do him well. It's not like Frank worked in the most relaxed setting. It was 1905, and Frank managed the dairy department at the Ionia Asylum for the Insane, a home to those with all types and levels of misunderstood mental illnesses and disorders and also criminals charged with "insanity." Frank accepted the time off. Besides, there was something he needed to do back home in Trenton, Michigan—kill a witch.

On May 15, 1905, Josephine Hammernick visited a nearby friend, and her husband, Michael, had a few drinks with the neighbor across the street from their small Third Street cottage in Trenton. Josephine came home before Michael, left an oil lamp burning on a table for him and made herself comfortable in bed. Around 10:10 p.m., Michael bid his neighbor goodnight and, while walking back home, saw a man run from his house. Michael tried to chase him down, but the man was much faster and was out of sight in no time. Out of breath and worried, Michael ran into his home and yelled for his wife. He heard her moan from their bedroom and found her slumped on the floor, leaning against a wall with a feather blanket over her.

"Are you OK? Are you sick? What's wrong?" he asked, but she just continued to groan and seemed to be in pain. Michael kneeled, put his hand on her chest and felt something wet. He stood up and ran toward their oil lamp and saw his hand was covered in blood. He brought the lamp back to the bedroom and found five bullet wounds in Josephine. Running outside,

Mich. State Reformatory, Ionia, Mich

An antique postcard of the reformatory at Ionia. *Author's collection.*

Michael screamed into the night, "Help! Help! My wife has been shot! She's been murdered!"

A doctor was called, but Josephine passed away before he arrived, unable to say even one word about what had happened. One bullet had entered her right arm, three were lodged in her chest and another just missed her left temple and eye. Her skull had been crushed, and her nose was broken, evidence of a possible struggle. None of the neighbors had heard gunfire, and it appeared the weapon was held close to the feather blanket around her, possibly muffling the sound of the shots. Josephine's body was taken away, and Michael was taken to the police station. With no actual witness to the crime, he was suspect number one, especially because he had been drinking that night. Police brought him to the station that night for questioning.

Frank Lesner was in Trenton the night of the murder. Sometime before midnight, he could have been found sitting at the bar of the lovely Hotel Felder, drinking a glass of water. There was nothing strange about him, nothing out of the ordinary. Frank calmly finished his water, went to his room and had a restful sleep. Leaving the hotel the next morning, he happened upon a patrolman walking the street. "Excuse me," Frank said to the officer. "I killed my godmother, Mrs. Hammernick," Frank said and then proceeded to give every detail of the crime, down to where he had thrown the gun. He said the reason for the murder was that she was a "witch" who had "bewitched his family" and had caused a lot of pain and suffering for them.

The crime felt so antiquated and misguided—not something someone from 1905 would do. Reporters jumped at the chance to interview Frank in jail. Everything about his character was perplexing, down to his orderly appearance and well-spoken manner. The tall twenty-six-year-old didn't look the part of a murderer with his large blue eyes and boyish looks. More shocking was how cold he was about the murder. County physician Isaac L. Polozker examined Frank and stated, "This is a remarkable case. While I don't think the man is in a normal condition, I would not say that he is not responsible. He is certainly a degenerate, but his manner and the connected story he tells would, I think, exclude him from that class of monomaniacs with a fixed idea."

"Frank, would you do it again?" asked one reporter. Frank stopped and looked deep in thought for a moment and said, "Yes, I think I would. I just did what I wanted to do, and I am willing to take the consequences."

"Then you don't feel sorry?" the reporter asked. Again, Frank took a moment to answer and said, "No, I don't believe I do." Next, the reporter asked what was on everyone's mind: "Do you believe in witches?"

"Certainly, I do," Frank declared.

"How was it that you came to the determination to rid the world of Mrs. Hammernick?"

Frank explained that ever since he was five years old, he could remember his father, John, telling stories about Josephine Hammernick, claiming he knew she was a witch and that she was the reason for all the family's problems. Frank didn't think too much of it. Josephine, after all, was his godmother, and as a child, he called her "Auntie." Frank had recently received a letter from his sister Augusta, informing him of his little sister Rose's strange affliction. She seemed to be suffering from rheumatism, or arthritis, and was in pain, which they thought strange for a girl in her late teens. A woman from Toledo was called up to examine Rose, and she arrived at the conclusion that the young girl was under the "influence of a witch." (Rosa passed away at the age of forty-five from sclerosis, so it's possible the disease was already exhibiting itself in her youth.) The woman even described where the "witch" lived, and the family agreed it was a perfect description of Josephine Hammernick's home in Trenton. "This is what determined me to kill her," Frank admitted.

Frank described the chaos that happened once he snuck inside the Hammernicks' home. He walked in through the back kitchen door. If Josephine had heard anything, she would have assumed it was her husband. Frank crept through the dimly lit house and walked into her bedroom. She screamed when she saw him, yelling in German, or what Frank referred to as "gibberish."

"I couldn't understand her, and wouldn't have stopped if I had. She threw the quilts over her head and yelled like a pig. Then I shot and shot until the yelling stopped and she lay still." When Frank was told Josephine was in fact not dead when he left her home, he said coldly, "Wasn't she? That's too bad. If I hadn't had enough bullets, I'd have gone out and got more. I'm glad she's gone." The *Detroit Free Press* described him as a "picture of unconcern when telling of the circumstances leading up to the murder."

As for Frank's personal vendetta with his godmother, not only had she hurt his family, but she had hurt his love life. He claimed relationships would be OK at first until the woman would "grow cold toward him." He said his "sweetheart" was Isabelle Lazette and that they had been engaged. When Isabelle heard what Frank said about her, she stated she had not seen him for over a year and that they were never engaged, although they

An old medieval woodcut of the stereotype of witches meeting the devil. *Public domain.*

had dated. She would have never believed Frank could be a murderer. She was shocked to learn what he had done and that there was a rumor going around that she had been "bewitched" by his godmother to dislike Frank. The only family to visit Frank while he was in jail were his two older brothers, Philip and John. They were horribly disappointed and embarrassed and offered to help Frank by sending him a lawyer and a priest. Frank seemed to show some remorse after their visit but just said, "I wish I had left it for someone else to do."

When John Lesner, Frank's father, was asked about the murder his son committed, John denied that he believed the family was bewitched, saying that the old neighborhood stories about the woman must have left an impression on his kids. But Rose Lesner gladly stated she believed she had been "bewitched," because her illness seemed to come out of nowhere. Furthermore, she said her hair had gotten so knotted up, they had to cut it off, another sure sign of witchcraft in her book when combined with the Toledo woman's diagnosis of "bewitchment." Frank never had a trial because four doctors declared him insane. Had Frank been diagnosed today, he most likely would have been labeled a sociopath with his lack of emotion and empathy, but that term did not come about until the 1930s. Four days after the murder, Frank was brought in front of a judge to face sentencing. The Trenton Village Hall was packed. Michael Hammernick sat down not far behind Frank, still reeling from the death of his wife. The session began, and the judge asked Frank to stand.

"How do you wish to plead to this charge of murder? Guilty or not guilty?"

"Well, I killed her all right, and pride myself that I made a good job of it, but don't know as I'm guilty of any crime." The absurdity of Frank's statement sent rage through Michael, who sprung from his seat and ran toward Frank but was quickly grabbed by an officer who told him, "Let the law deal with him, Mike," and led him to sit down. Michael was lucky that Frank had confessed. Without that confession, it was possible the law would have jailed Michael longer on circumstantial evidence. On June 19, 1905, Frank was escorted back to the Ionia Asylum but this time as a prisoner, not an employee. Not a single family member or friend showed up to see him off. His sentence was for life, and he was considered dangerous to the public. As he left Trenton, he said, "I'm glad I did it."

Frank's family was not alone in their belief that there were real witches doing devious work against others in southeast Michigan. The murder fired up a lot of people, who offered their advice on how to deal with pesky witches. One woman believed all Frank had to do to break the curse was shoot a silver bullet at a photograph of the witch. The *Detroit Free Press* noted a sudden rise in people offering their services to "break the spell of witches" after the murder—for a cost, of course.

PRISON BREAK

On September 12, 1908, Frank Lesner and three other convicts broke free from the confines of the Ionia Asylum. The men had obviously planned their escape for months and had carved a key from a common table knife. During their routine exercise, the men used their makeshift key to escape through a basement door. Frank threatened a security guard with a knife, and he had no choice but to let the men escape or possibly lose his own life. The other three escapees were Hiram McCaffrey, who was in for larceny; James Swane, who was committed for attempted robbery; and Fred Clark, who was doing time for burglary. None of the men had any discernible characteristics that made them stand out in a crowd, besides Frank being a tall man. They were all described as being perfectly capable of carrying on a normal and sane conversation unless certain things were brought up to Frank—perhaps the topic of witches.

Interior of Walls, Michigan Reformatory, Ionia, Mich.   Pub. by Ionia Post Card Co., Ionia, Mich.

An antique postcard of the reformatory/prison at Ionia. *Author's collection.*

After Frank's escape, Trenton was put on high alert, and the police were extra vigilant. It was believed that Frank would try to see his family or even seek further revenge on the Hammernick family. One woman could have sworn she saw Frank get on a train. Maybe he did in fact make it back home to see family and tell them of his plans. If he did, the family never said anything about it, and Frank vanished—or did he?

FINDING FRANK

Going through genealogical records, an old military pension card for Frank Lesner existed and had something very strange written on it—the word *alias*. As can be seen from the photograph, "alias" is crossed off next to the name Daniel Danning and added below to the name Frank Lesner. A search for Daniel Danning revealed that he appeared sometime after 1908 around Angola in Steuben County, Indiana. A marriage record census shows Daniel Danning married Marian S. Clark in July 1909, and a few more suspicious details emerge. His birthday is listed as June 15, 1878, the same as Frank Lesner's. Marriage certificates list the names of the couple's parents, and Danning's says that his parents are John and Julia, the same names as Frank's parents, although Daniel's future records list his parents as sometimes being born in New York and Ireland, while Frank's parents were born in Germany. According to a July 21, 1909, article in the *Steuben Republican*, the couple was married at Marian's parents' home. It does not mention any close relatives of Daniel's being at the ceremony, just a man named Arthur Thomas, who was the best man.

Marian and Daniel were married until the end of 1919, when a divorce was granted to Marian after she asked for one in 1916 on the grounds of "cruel and inhumane treatment," stating Daniel forced hard farm labor on her and refused to provide fuel to heat their home or to cook with. Their only child, born on September 28, 1916, died at two months old, which probably didn't help their volatile relationship. Daniel was remarried again in March 1922 to Rachel Audra Wiggins, and they stayed married, raising seven children around Steuben County, Indiana.

The final piece possibly connecting Danning and Lesner is the fact that they both served in the military at the same time. Frank Lesner served in Company I, Thirtieth United States Volunteer Infantry in the Philippines from July 1899 until April 1901, when he was discharged, most likely for contracting malaria, and sent home. On November 8, 1940, Daniel Danning passed away from an illness at the age of sixty-two. His obituary mentions

A military pension card. *Courtesy of the National Archives.*

the very same military credentials as Frank Lesner's. A look at the records for that military unit does not contain the name Daniel Danning, but it does contain the name Frank Lesner. As for the name Daniel Danning being on the military pension card, it's possible he had tried to apply for pension money if there was anything to receive, but perhaps he had to step back for fear of revealing too much about himself and his notorious status as an escaped prisoner and convicted cold-blooded murderer.

Furthermore, Daniel's obituary does not contain the names of any family members, past or present, besides those of his wife, Rachel, and their children. A World War I draft card for Daniel described him as being tall with blue eyes and brown hair, which also matched Frank's description. Without some hidden confession found tucked away in an attic, this is only speculation, but it is highly probable speculation. The years after Frank escaped prison still allowed a person to easily take on another identity and hide in plain sight. Records like social security numbers or even fingerprints were not in existence. Someone could make up a completely new life story for themselves, and people just had to believe it if they had no reason to think otherwise. If Frank Lesner assumed the alias Daniel Danning and if the two men are in fact the same person, it appears that for over one hundred years, Frank Lesner got away with his escape—until now.

13

THE DEVIL IN DETROIT

On the morning of Wednesday, November 8, 1905, the people living near Herman Menz's Stanton Avenue home in Detroit's west side woke up to something peculiar—a fourteen-foot-tall statue of what appeared to be Satan glaring down from behind a pulpit right next to Herman's house and flush with the wooden sidewalk. Children on their way to school were the first to take notice and gawk, which caused adults to stop and stare, which led to a much larger crowd of curious and outraged citizens as the day went on. Clearly, Herman Menz wanted to make a statement, because not only could the statue's head be seen two streets over, but at eye level, carved into the eight-foot-tall base was a statement in Latin that, when translated, read:

> *Man is not created, but*
> *is developed.*
> *God did not make man,*
> *but man did make the gods.*

Herman Menz was a stonemason by trade with a workshop in his side yard. People walking by could constantly hear his tools clanking away as he carved tombstones and other stone projects. His two-story wooden home was already adorned with stone dragon heads on its corners, but no one knew how to process his latest lawn decoration. Neighbors were "incensed" and thought it was "an insult to the community," believing that a monument worshipping Satan had been erected among them.

Hypocrisy Everywhere

Within just two days of unveiling his statue, the "Menz Devil," as the press named it, became national and international news. The once calm street quickly descended into madness as thousands of Detroiters came to see "the devil." The statue's stone muscles were no match for the "mob of excited boys," who "gathered like a horde of indignant iconoclasts intent on destroying the sculptured Satan" and who took stones from Herman's stone yard and hurled them while yelling, "Lop his old head off!" A wad of tobacco chew became stuck in its eye at one point, and mud was spattered across its surface.

Described as a "short, stout, man" with white hair, a bushy mustache, thick glasses and a German accent, Herman began patrolling the front of his house while holding a large stick to protect his property. The statue had already suffered damage and was cracked and chipped in spots. The police took over at night to keep the vandalism at bay.

Herman knew his creation would cause a stir, and that was most likely his goal, whether he admitted it or not. He claimed he built the statue because it "amused him." The press remarked that Herman was getting a kick out of the excitement around the statue and noted there was a "twinkle in his eye" and a smile on his elderly face, but he was taken aback by the dramatic reactions and even threats he had received. Herman pointed out there were far more grotesque-looking monsters carved into the local Gothic-inspired churches, such as Detroit's Fort Street Presbyterian Church or Saint John's Episcopal on Woodward Avenue.

The front of Herman Menz's house and the notorious statue. *Public domain.*

Reporters wanted to know what prompted Herman to put the shocking statue up in the first place. It was obvious he didn't just install the statue thinking it would benefit his curb appeal. The idea may have started with the Welsh revival tent meetings that were going on in his neighborhood and being allowed to use city property free of charge. The meetings attracted a lot of people, were loud and sometimes ran late into the evening. He petitioned the city council to stop the meetings, but his complaints didn't achieve anything. He felt the local churches needed to pay property taxes and pull event permits, just like regular citizens and businesses. Herman saw hypocrisy everywhere in the world, and it was frustrating to him. He was a man who liked to see progress and was interested in local politics. He thought sidewalks should be made of cement, not wood, and was vocal about streetcars extending into other parts of Detroit to make it easier for people to get downtown. Good ideas aside, Herman was sometimes dismissed and considered "eccentric" because he was an "infidel," a word commonly used to describe an atheist in the early nineteenth century.

From a young age, Herman had declared himself atheist after having bad experiences with religion. "I have had some hard ups and downs in the seventy-one years I have been in this world," he told reporters. "And the hardest knocks I ever got were from persons who professed to be good Christians. They were that kind who put a sanctimonious look on their face, turn one eye toward heaven and the other toward your pocket. There is no religion in the church today. It is all business. I have lived in Germany and in England, and while I find hypocrites in the church all over, I find more in this country than in any other."

Reporters interviewed neighbors, eager to get details about the little stonecutter's character, and surprisingly learned many of them thought he was a nice man but was just strong in his convictions. For trying to take a stand, some citizens even commended his act and thought of him as brave and truthful, while others thought he had been sent to Detroit by the devil himself. Resident Sol Cohen stated, "The only difference between Mr. Menz and the rest of us, is that he flaunts his unbelief to the public gaze; we aren't so bold, but most of us share his views."

Herman was more than happy to talk to reporters and share his opinions and views on religion. Never short of controversial statements, Herman told the *Detroit Free Press*, "The devil is the best friend of the ministers, I say. If there was no devil and everybody did what was right all the time, the ministers would have to get out and earn their bread and butter as other people do."

After a few nights of constant crowds, reporters and warding off vandals, Herman was exhausted and looked it. In the hopes he could get people to just calm down or lose interest, he wrapped the statue up to cover and protect it, but the people still gathered, so he removed his statue from the pedestal and completely out of public view. He sarcastically stated that his "devil was now in purgatory." Herman awoke in the morning to crowds "gathered in the vicinity, hooting, howling and calling upon his infernal majesty to appear." To enact some type of crowd control, the police, half joking, half serious, suggested he charge admission to see the statue. Herman saw it as a possible solution to the problem and promptly pulled a permit with the city for his "event."

STEP RIGHT UP AND SEE THE DEVIL!

On November 12, 1905, the stone celebrity stared idly on as thousands of people lined up, each paying ten cents to earn the bragging right that they had gazed upon the hideous satanic statue crafted by the devil-worshiper himself, Herman Menz (or whatever story they wanted to tell people to justify paying money to stare at a statue). A minister named D.H. Glass even disguised himself so he could get a close-up look at the statue. And after visiting Trinity Episcopal Church to compare, he decided the gargoyles at the church were far more horrendous looking than Menz's sculpture.

The line never shrank, and even Detroit's wealthy elite showed up to see what all the fuss was about, including one of the "finest automobiles in Detroit" carrying James E. Scripps, a newspaper mogul and founder of the Detroit Art Museum (which later became the Detroit Institute of Art). Scripps felt the statue was worthy of a museum collection, especially because of the controversy surrounding it and the message Herman Menz wished to convey. Scripps offered to buy it, but Herman refused to sell, which put his integrity on display. It was reported that a couple of other offers had come in from Chicago, which Herman also refused.

Charging for admission worked, and the throngs of people eventually faded and interest subsided, but that didn't mean people were any less offended by what Herman had done. There were groups that had threatened him to remove the blasphemous statue, "or else they would," and rather suspiciously, around the end of December 1905, Warren West from Ypsilanti claimed he had carved the statue and had never been paid for his work. Herman admitted Warren had made the base of the statue but was adamant he had not carved the figure; he never revealed the artist's identity out of concern the negative attention would affect his job. "Warren West can't carve any better than his dog!" Herman spat back. He argued that Warren

STATUE OF THE DEVIL AND DETROIT MAN WHO BUILT IT.

Left: An image from the *Spokane Press*, November 15, 1905. *Public domain.*

Below: An antique postcard. *Courtesy of the Detroit Historical Society.*

"Inferno", Electric Park, Detroit, Mich.

was trying to run a con on him after he had docked his pay after he broke something on a job site some time ago. Herman claimed that Warren wasn't even a true sculptor but a common laborer. Warren is listed in the Ypsilanti city directories as a stonecutter from 1901 to 1907, but before and after that, his occupation is listed as a carpenter and, later, a gardener. Sculptor or not, Warren showed up with a writ of replevin, which is a legal means by which to reclaim property.

The once scandalous statue, now damaged and cemented back together in many places, was dumped on a cart and hauled off, much to the protest of Herman. According to author George W. Stark, the statue was "imprisoned in the basement of the county building, oddly enough, in a room beneath the county morgue." On January 2, 1906, the statue was auctioned off to Arthur H. Gaukler. A large crowd showed up, and the bids were heated until the gavel locked in place the final price of $40, around $1,100 today. Gaukler owned Electric Park, Detroit's first ever amusement park, that featured shows, roller coasters, games and more and operated from 1906 to 1928 near Belle Isle. A castle-like building was created specifically to house the statue and featured a maze. Once a person got to the center, the "devil" would be waiting with eerie lights for dramatic effect, and an additional three-tined spear was added to the statue for extra flair. The attraction was called "Inferno: Menz Devil" and for almost three years, the statue lived within its attraction until Gaukler decided it was a "hoodoo," blaming the statue for low attendance on weekends. After the attraction was removed, George Stark wrote, "There are old-timers who insist that on the spot where the devil once reigned in all his majesty, a lilac bush now blossoms every springtime in his memory." In the fall of 1908, Menz's devil was once again back home with Herman.

To celebrate the return of his little stone friend and his seventy-second birthday, on November 1, Herman and his friends had a party and put the statue back on its pedestal (now set twelve feet away from the road) and covered him with a veil, which they pulled off at 8:00 p.m. to a small gathering. The moment was more of a novelty, with the *Detroit Free Press* writing, "Herman Menz, devil-maker, resurrected his Satanic majesty last night." A new, more dramatic message intended to ruffle feathers was on the new pedestal and read:

> *Hail to thee Satan, arch-rebel against truth, Hail to thee*
> *Avenger of reason downtrod. With laurel we crown thee, as*
> *Victor we greet thee, who vanished Jehovah, the priest-made God.*

The whole thing was still entertaining to Herman, but the second coming of his devil statue caused nowhere near the commotion that the first had in 1905. Dr. Tobias Sigel, a good friend of Herman's, saved many of the newspaper articles and letters of support (and hate) Herman received over his statue. He kept everything in a scrapbook that is stored in the Joseph A. Labadie Collection at the Special Collections Research Center of the University of Michigan.

One positive piece of fan mail read:

Dear Sir,

I did not believe that there was in America one free and independent man until I saw in the papers that you erected a monument against human ignorance and imbecility. Let me congratulate and admire you. But remember, you are an exception among the flock of slaves around you and that they may unite against you. Show them that if men were really independent, they would be good to each other in the first place and that a few scores of fearless men or women who would stand out for progress like giants among the 80 million grasshoppers that populate this country would do much to promote moral and intellectual improvement. Show that morality is man's true nature and that existing religion is only man's hypocrisy and insincerity.

Yours truly,
C. Chassang

Most interesting in the scrapbook is a party invite titled "Unveiling of the Devil at Mr. Herman Menz's home, 308 Stanton Ave., on his 71st birthday, November 5, 1905." Just a few days before Herman's story would be heard around the world, Menz and his other "free thinker" friends were having a good laugh about the statue and probably wondering how the public would receive it—not even ready for just how crazy things would get.

Herman Menz passed away from pneumonia on September 27, 1919, at the age of eighty-four. His wife died in 1912 from cancer, and afterward, he retired and moved to Farmington Hills. He appeared from time to time in the papers, one time after getting pickpocketed, and another time, he appeared in the news for refusing to swear on the Bible in court.

After wondering whatever became of Detroit's infamous devil statue, Malcolm W. Bingay, the managing editor of the *Detroit Free Press*, wrote on May 30, 1948, "Herman Menz deserves a better place in our history than

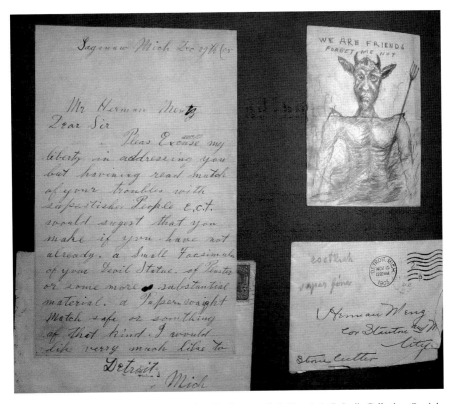

An image from Dr. Tobias Sigel's scrapbook. *Courtesy of the Joseph A. Labadie Collection, Special Collections Research Center, University of Michigan Library.*

an unrecorded notation in the limbo of municipal oblivion." In George Stark's 1939 book, *In Old Detroit*, he wrote about the whereabouts of the statue, "The best authorities on these obscure matters will tell you that old Herman Menz's Devil now dwells privately and quite alone on a farm in St. Clare County." Menz's Devil is still out there somewhere—if not physically, at least metaphorically.

14

THE SUMMER OF THE MONSTER

The cozy and quaint tourist destination of Sister Lakes in Van Buren County wasn't prepared for the exciting and terrifying turn of events June 1964 would bring to the small town. The popular resort area has ten lakes within a six-mile radius: Round Lake, Big Crooked Lake, Little Crooked Lake, Magician Lake, Dewey Lake and Cable Lake. The locals were used to welcoming vacationers, fishermen, campers and boaters every summer. But the last thing on anyone's minds was the arrival of an entirely different type of tourist—a monster.

Thirty-three-year-old Evelyn Utrup called the police on June 9, 1964. She knew her phone call would be one of the strangest ones received that evening. Evelyn and her husband owned a farm, and two of their farmworkers, Gordon Brown and Joseph Smith, saw something in the shadows that shook them to their core. That night, while leaving the farm on Garret Road near Topash Street, their car headlights illuminated a large form. Gordon's and Joseph's eyes widened in horror as they tried to make sense of what they were seeing. In the beams of light was a dark, hairy creature, easily nine feet tall, standing still among the farm buildings. Both men were experienced hunters and knew that whatever they were looking at was not any native Michigan animal they had ever seen.

When police arrived that evening, Evelyn Utrup told them she had recently been outside behind her farmhouse when she, too, had a strange experience. She had heard something running toward her in the dark. The footsteps were so loud and heavy and it scared her so much that she ran into the house, slammed and locked the door and listened while her dogs barked wildly and chased whatever had been lurking in the darkness. Evelyn had been too terrified to look back when she ran and wasn't able to give any physical descriptions, but she said she "felt saved by her dogs." According to a report in the *Holland Sentinel*, her dog Chester came back from his heroic chase with a swollen eye that took a month to heal. Oddly enough, police found unusually large footprints behind Evelyn's home that measured six inches at the ball of the foot, with a four-inch-wide heel, and looked human-like in shape. Even Evelyn's husband said he saw large, reflective eyes staring at him from behind a bush one night.

A drawing of the Sister Lakes monster based on witness descriptions.
Illustration by Amberrose Hammond.

The Utrups and their farmworkers had not been the only people to see something peculiar. Other residents from the Sister Lakes area had made police reports describing a black, furry, five-hundred-pound, nine-foot-tall, leathery-faced monster with reflective, glowing eyes. Some reports claimed the creature made a sound like a "goose honking" or, even more disturbing, a "baby crying." By June 11, Cass County undersheriff Ernie Kraus said ten people had made monster reports, but this wasn't the first batch the police had received. Reports of a dark-haired beast had been trickling into the department for a few years during the summer months. However, now saddled with more monster sightings than ever before, the police had to act and make sure a potentially dangerous animal wasn't on the loose.

A nighttime search of the Utrup farm and nearby woods was organized the following evening on June 10. Armed with rifles and flashlights, the police turned monster hunters hoped their flashlights would connect with the creature's signature reflective eyes, but the hunt was abruptly cut short. News of the creature sightings had spread fast. As police tried to conduct their search, they were interrupted by endless curiosity seekers and amateur monster hunters. The officers had to give up the search and start directing traffic, as over two hundred cars drove into the normally quiet area. Extra officers from nearby Van Buren County had to come help direct the overwhelming surge of people who were hoping to catch a glimpse of the creature from the safety of their car, treating the area like some type of drive-through zoo exhibit.

News sources jumped at the chance to report, often sarcastically, on Michigan's bizarre moment. The *News-Palladium* from Benton Harbor asked, "Who weighed the monster" to know it weighed five hundred pounds and suggested whatever the farmworkers Brown and Smith saw was most likely human, and they were just ignorant. The reporter snidely wrote, "It has a leathery face, but farmworkers are hardly noted for peaches-and-cream complexions." The media named the creature the "Sister Lakes Monster" and the "Monster of Dewey Lake," as many of the sightings were around that body of water.

GOOD MORNING, MONSTER

On Thursday, June 11, at 9:15 a.m., thirteen-year-old Joyce Smith and sisters Patsy and Gail Clayton, twelve and thirteen years old, claimed they saw the monster in daylight on Swisher Street and Town Hall Road in Silver Creek Township while taking a walk. The creature emerged from the woods on the side of the road. Gail fainted on the spot but was quickly revived by the other girls, and the monster retreated into the woods. They ran to a nearby house, and the police were notified. Dowagiac Police Chief Richard Wild received the call and immediately sent armed officers to the area the girls claimed they saw the creature in. A state police plane was even scheduled to fly over the area. Gail Clayton told reporters that the creature "did not look like a man." Patsy was the closest to the monster and said, "It looked like a bear" and "was about seven to nine feet tall and had a black face."

Different theories circulated about what the creature could logically be other than a bona fide monster. Everything from an elk, a bear, a horse and even an escaped circus gorilla were considered. The most likely option was a large bear that had wandered into the area from northern Michigan, something not terribly common at that time but not impossible. The *Herald-Press* from St. Joseph reported, "Some longtime residents say the swampy area northwest of Dowagiac is a prime huckleberry region and that the monster likely is a bear, a deer or maybe even some elk, which reportedly escaped from a farm pasture along M60 about three years ago." If the creature was indeed a misplaced animal, it seems people who had experienced a sighting would have been able to identify it as such. While a bear could stand on two legs, it wouldn't be common for an elk or deer to walk on their hind legs. "That many people can't be wrong, so there must be something out there. This has been going on for about two weeks, but people have been reluctant to call because it's a fantastic story and they're afraid of ridicule. I think there's a logical explanation. I think it's an animal," Deputy Sheriff Ernest Kraus told reporters.

THIS MONSTER MEANS BUSINESS

National headlines declaring, "Michigan Hunts Monster" and "Monster Terrorizes Area, Ties up Traffic" captured the attention of Americans and Michiganders. Savvy business owners capitalized on the moment, and by Saturday, June 13, local businesses saw an increase in sales thanks to the influx of people. "Special Monster Kits" for $7.95 were sold at Harvey's East General Store. The kit consisted of a mallet, one arrow, a baseball bat and a net for that quick and easy capture after the monster had been knocked unconscious by the bat. A flashlight was also included because what serious monster hunter works during the day? The Dowagiac Theater offered a horror movie double feature. Local restaurant specials featured "Monster Burgers" and "Monster Sandwiches." And diners were meant to wash those down with a "Monster Beer." Gas prices also increased locally, with some stations advertising "Get-Away" gasoline, in case a motorist needed to make a quick escape after a monster encounter.

The dramatic attention and additional surplus of people didn't sit well with the locals. Fences on private properties had been knocked over, crops had been trampled on and Swisher Road by Dewey Lake was completely littered with trash from careless people. A newspaper reporter camped out one evening and counted thirty different cars in just fifteen minutes casing the backroads. Gawkers would even stop and pester locals, asking where they could find the monster, as if it had an address and telephone number. Headlights from the excess traffic shined into homes at all hours of the night. Even more alarming, many of these thrill-seekers were carrying loaded guns. Three teens from Detroit were caught "monster hunting" with a .375 H&H magnum handgun, and a group of baseball bat–wielding kids was chased out of the woods by police. Clearly, they were putting their "Special Monster Kits" into action. A farmer even reported that someone took a couple of shots at his black Shetland pony, thankfully missing. The local chamber of commerce was getting annoyed. They weren't sure if this was the kind of attention they wanted to see continue. Some residents laughed the whole debacle off, including the existence of the monster, but some residents took a few extra precautions, just in case, and made sure their shotguns were loaded and within arm's reach in case a large, hairy beast should decide to invade their property. Police said many women in the area were not leaving their homes without a male companion to protect them. Not only were some residents genuinely worried, but a few migrant workers in the strawberry fields quit their jobs after hearing about the monster. Some workers literally had to be "prodded" to go back into the fields, with one farmer stating, "This was a joke at first, but it's not a joke anymore. We've lost a lot of berries because of the 'monster.'"

Jack Hadley, a local beer distributor, exacerbated the moment after he offered a $1,000 reward for the "live" capture of the creature. People had until 5:00 p.m. on June 22 to present the monster's body and collect the reward, but Cass County sheriff Robert Dool quickly shut the contest down. With the number of guns and weapons people were carrying, the sheriff felt the reward money could put people in a dangerous situation. Deputy Andy Chavous stated, "I'd feel safer if it was just me and the monster," after police stopped a car filled with eight teenagers "armed with tire irons and clubs" one night.

By day five of the excitement, no new reports had been made, and things were starting to simmer down. The trail of cars was thinning, and interest was waning. The monster was still front-page news by the end of the week, but now a new monster had been spotted near Ionia in Kent County. Nineteen-year-old Wayne Ritter and his seventeen-year-old brother, Lloyd, were on their way to Grand Haven from Lansing around 4:00 a.m. when they witnessed a "hairy, gorilla-like creature about ten feet tall with a shuffling gait" cross the I-96 Highway near Saranac. The brothers talked to the Kent County Sheriff's Department for one hour, and the sighting was taken seriously. With all the excitement around the Sister Lakes area, maybe the "monster" had moved north. An officer went to the area to check things out, but nothing was found at first. The next day, on June 18, State Trooper Richard Abbott and his tracking dog Jocko were driving down I-96 at 2:00 a.m. when he saw what he thought was a deer jump in front of the car ahead of him. When he realized it wasn't a deer and could possibly be the monster, he pulled over and bravely gave chase, but heavy rain started to pour down, causing the officer and the dog to lose track of their monster after it crawled over a fence.

Trooper Abbott found "hair that looked more like it had been pulled from a dead hide than live skin" on the fence the thing had crawled over, along with a glove. Whoever the monster was, it was very much a human pulling a prank. Another monster sighting turned out to be eight teens "walking piggyback" with a black poncho over them just west of Ionia along highway M-21. A motorist reported them to the police, and they were picked up and given a lecture at the jail.

The *Holland Evening Sentinel* reported that Sister Lakes merchants felt "it was the greatest thing that's happened in these parts since the advent of electric light." The extra cash injection was a welcome boon. When the dust settled, a few business owners actually missed the "monster madness." But still, some concerned citizens decided to put their homes for sale and moved out of an area that was possibly inhabited by an unknown monster. By the end of June 1964, the monster and reports of it all seemed to vanish and became just another entertaining and novel moment in the area's past.

WAS IT BIGFOOT?

Bigfoot, Sasquatch, Yeti and Yowie are names from different cultures around the world that all describe the same thing—a large, hairy, human-like, upright-walking creature that has been spotted all over the planet for centuries or more. Could the residents who saw the Sister Lakes monster have encountered this legendary creature? The 1960s were considered a golden era for Bigfoot, with pioneering researchers John Green, Ivan T. Sanderson and René Dahinden gathering firsthand accounts of encounters with the mysterious creatures and taking a serious look at the phenomenon. Many people have been reluctant to share their Bigfoot experiences for fear of ridicule, including many Sister Lakes residents who probably never came forward. What was rather interesting and a little spooky about the Sister Lakes monster was the reported sounds the creature made. The sound of a "goose honking" or a "baby crying" is a characteristic that has shown up in Bigfoot research. Some Bigfoot researchers theorize the creature has the vocal ability to mimic sounds exceptionally well, known as "vocal mimicry." Sounding like a goose can help shield its identity, or perhaps mimicking the cries of a human baby can serve as a lure to some unsuspecting human. So the next time you vacation at the Sister Lakes, maybe keep a lookout for a pair of large, glowing eyes watching you from the woods, or bring your own Monster Hunters Kit—you know, just in case.

15

THE MYSTERIOUS LIFE AND TIMES OF MARIAN SPORE BUSH

Marian Spore Bush was a young child when images and warnings of the future came to her in dreams. At the age of four, she awoke from a nightmare of a scary, haggard-looking man coming to her school and waving a knife, making threats to the children. The next day at school, her dream became a reality when the same man from her dream showed up, and the scene played out like her dream had been a dress rehearsal. The kids were so shaken from the event that the teacher sent everyone home for the day. When she was older, she dreamed of a large passenger ship being attacked, and shortly after, the RMS *Lusitania* was struck by a German U-boat on May 7, 1915, killing 1,198 people. It wasn't always pleasant and welcome to have these strange abilities, but they would one day take Marian on a journey from being a popular dentist to becoming a world-renowned painter guided by the hands of unseen spirits.

Born Flora Marian Spore in Bay City, Michigan, on October 22, 1878, Marian was the oldest of three children. She had a younger brother, James, and a little sister named Sarabelle. Intelligent and bright, at just sixteen years old, Marian was accepted into the University of Michigan and studied literature there for a year before moving on to the school of dentistry. She graduated in 1899, one of only a few women enrolled in the program. Fresh out of school and supplied with a glowing recommendation from the top dental professors at the University of Michigan, she got a position as a dental assistant with Dr. Eugene W. Light in Saginaw. The following year, in March 1900, she opened her own practice in her hometown of Bay City at the age of twenty-two. She was Bay County's first female dentist and quickly became one of the most popular dentists in town, able to afford two dental assistants for her office.

Statistically, dentistry is a profession with a high suicide rate. To add to that fact, Marian's first employer, Dr. Light, killed himself in 1903 at the age of sixty-two by drinking carbolic acid, but Marian truly enjoyed the work and seemed perfectly suited to the meticulous and mechanical precision the job required. She was confident in her ability, loved that she could set her own hours and felt it was the perfect profession for women who didn't want to step into marriage or raise a family right away, if at all. She said, "No girl should think of attempting this work who isn't strong physically and mentally and who doesn't love the profession." The book *Women of Bay County* states that Marian was known for her "progressive and excellent work in the day when she fabricated inlays, crowns, bridgework and dental plates in her own laboratory. She was also a pioneer in the field of periodontal dentistry."

ALL THINGS MUST CHANGE

On May 29, 1919, almost twenty years into her career, everything in Marian's successful life came to an abrupt halt. Her mother, Helen, who she was extremely close with, had been suffering from heart problems and passed away at home at the age of fifty-eight. Helen always told her daughter that if she was somehow able to make contact with the living after she died, she'd try to do something so Marian would know she was still with her in spirit.

Marian wished her mother would appear to her as a full apparition, like the kind she read about in stories, but as time went on without any apparition or communication whatsoever, Marian took matters into her own hands. Skeptical by nature, she started to investigate the different methods of spirit communication. There was no way she was going to one of the many mediums who advertised their services in Bay City. She considered most of them to be charlatans.

In 1919, Ouija boards were all the rage, enjoying a revival after World War I. Curious about what a square piece of wood with letters and numbers printed on it could do for her, Marian found one buried in the toy section of a local department store. Once home, she read the directions and felt deflated. First, the instructions read "it was a game," and second, it "took two people to play." Contacting her mother via a "game" seemed insulting to her memory, and she tossed the board aside, embarrassed she even considered using it.

A few months later, a strange article in the August 20, 1919 *Bay City Times* caught Marian's attention. Some people onboard a yacht that was cruising northern Lake Huron were using a Ouija board for entertainment when a surprising message came through. A man claimed he had been "crushed to death" and seemed confused about his newfound existence. He came up three different times during the cruise with similar names—Harrison Maleir or Harris Villaire. While their boat was docked at Sault Ste. Marie, the boaters sent a letter with a self-addressed stamped envelope to the *Bay City Times*'s office requesting any information on people recently killed in accidents. They were shocked to learn that whoever was speaking through the board had told the truth. Seventy-three-year-old Harrison Maleir had been struck and killed by a car in Bay City on the evening of August 3. Even stranger, Marian was out driving that evening and had witnessed Maleir get hit on the corner of Fifth and Water Streets. That was enough evidence for her to take the board seriously. If the spirit of someone recently killed could communicate with completely random people on a boat, maybe she could indeed receive a message from her mother. It "took two to play," so her father, Melvin, indulged her and became a willing participant in the experiment. Father and daughter placed their hands on the wooden planchette, the little heart-shaped device that points to characters on the board. Under their light touch, it effortlessly started to move across the board. They blamed each other for moving it, but neither one claimed the movement. Like magic, the board spelled out things that had only been between Marian and her mother. She had communication at last.

Her mother would mention the nice little things she saw her sister do with her daughter. Sarabelle was always able to back these statements up as fact. Rather humorously, her mother came through with a message for their housekeeper. "Tell Mrs. Pollack to stop eating the lonesome meals—the brown heavy things are making her ill." Turns out, she had been eating doughnuts daily with tea, which was upsetting her stomach. She stopped and felt better.

As Marian continued to use the board, she found she could get messages on her own after her sister excused herself during a session to grab a blanket. Marian's hands were still on the planchette when it suddenly started moving with only her hand on it. It moved in all directions and spelled everything from dates, facts and even what appeared to be gossip.

As her use with the board progressed, Marian could feel a difference between who was leaving messages. Her mother's energy and presence became easy for her to recognize, but then there were the other more "mischievous" messages that she learned to ignore, especially after the advice made her feel like a fool. The board told her she would be going to New York City soon, and it was correct. She got an invite from her brother James Spore, who was a lieutenant in the U.S. Navy, to come to celebrate with him on board the ship that he had been made commander of. The board told her to bring all kinds of unnecessary clothes, even the bridesmaid dress she wore at her brother's wedding. When she arrived with all the extra trunks of clothes that she never used during her stay, everyone had a good laugh, but she felt ridiculous.

Marian believed that if someone was unbalanced, they shouldn't mess with talking to spirits. In her autobiography, *They*, she wrote, "I wish to state that unless one is well balanced and can look at things in a straight, practical way, weighing and separating reasons until all is satisfactorily accounted for, psychic communication is most dangerous. It is terrifying if misunderstood—a fearsome experience on which to embark." When she got back from New York, her extra luggage in tow, she wondered how it was that such good information could come through, yet such bad and sometimes troubling messages could be part of the mix. She felt there were two types of souls. The entities giving bad advice and playing jokes were people who died but didn't want to move on to a different level. She learned they are typically the first spirit a person encounters when trying to establish communication with the other side.

The second type were helpful spirits that were above the trickery. They told Marian to keep working with them and that she would soon be able to ignore the lesser spirits. She only needed to focus her intention on the good coming through. In time, she became more aware of what the good and bad felt like while using the board. The bad spirits always said things that were familiar to her or stated numbers and facts. Marian felt the good spirits didn't use names or exact dates. They had moved on from Earth and had started to forget the unimportant details. When her mother first came through the board, she used names but eventually stopped and started using descriptions, such as "the sad-faced girl" for the housekeeper and "the happy-faced girl" for her little sister. Marian felt this was because her mother's spirit was evolving to a higher plane. By improving her discernment, Marian felt like she had made a breakthrough.

Eventually, she was told she didn't have to rely on the Ouija board anymore to communicate, so she picked up a writing planchette. Similar to the planchette of the Ouija board, the top peg has a pencil, and when moved across paper, it is able to write. One day while using the writing planchette, the spirits asked if she wanted to have something drawn for her, something "pretty." Marian had never had an art lesson in her life, but the idea of letting a spirit draw using her hand intrigued her. Her mother claimed she had found something for Marian to alleviate the depression she had been in since her death.

Images came through the writing planchette, and eventually, Marian was told to just pick up a normal pencil and let them guide her hand. She did 275 pencil sketches in the first year alone. After that, she was directed to move on to oil paints on large canvases. Marian said, "They do not wish me to make small paintings. They seem to require large spectacular canvases, which will attract attention to the message They have to convey, by showing how They can work through me, thus demonstrating that They live, think and devise motifs and technique simply to prove that there is no Death."

The word *They* is always capitalized in her autobiography, and "They" is what she called the spirit collective that guided her throughout the rest of her life. Sometimes, a spirit would step forward and introduce itself. One of the spirits Marian worked with was said to be that of Gustave Doré, the famous French illustrator and engraver who died in 1883. Doré laid claim to anything "gruesome or horrifying" in her paintings. Marian claimed to know absolutely nothing about the artist.

"They" would start a painting by moving Marian's arm up and down, left and right on the canvas, which sometimes took a long time. She had no idea what the painting being mapped out by spirit guidance was going to look like. As she learned, some paintings were scrapped or painted over if her guides didn't think it looked right. "There is nothing weird, uncanny or strange about all this," Marian said. "They simply give me these directions, and I receive them with the inner hearing—the way They converse 'over there.' To me, it is simplicity itself, not at all unnatural, except that I am guided by their thoughts inducted to my perception, and these same thoughts take possession of the brain cells that actuate my hands. It is simply telepathy between my mind and the minds of these People."

Wanting more proof of their existence, she once asked them if they could be photographed. Their response was, "Extend your thumb and forefinger as far apart as possible and imagine the distance between to be as high as the soul of the tallest man. We will say the soul is standing there. Now press the thumb and forefinger together as closely as possible—so tightly that it hurts—and the soul still is between them. What is there to photograph?"

Dentist by day and now artist by night, Marian needed to talk to someone about what she was experiencing and reached out to Yale graduate Dr. Walter Franklin Prince of the American Psychical Research Society, a group formed in 1884 by leading thinkers and scientists of the day for the purpose of applying serious study to paranormal subjects. Marian wrote letters and made trips to New York City to show him her work in person.

Impressed with everything about Marian's story, Dr. Prince introduced her early paintings to Professor Arthur Wesley Dow, the head of the Fine Arts Department at Columbia University. Dow and Prince evaluated her paintings, and Dow admitted that if she wanted to make money by painting, she would do well, which was encouraging to her. Dr. Prince asked her to keep notes on her abilities and send them to him. She also recorded forty-five dreams she had among other experiences and messages she received from her "controls," as they were first called.

At something of a crossroads in her life, Marian had a decision to make—continue her life as it was or devote her life to art, painting and this unseen and exciting world that had welcomed her into its circle. Through art, she had released trapped grief from her mother's death, and she felt so wonderful that she wanted to give that feeling back to others who were in need of it. After much thought, she closed the doors of her successful Bay City dentistry practice of twenty-one years in 1921 and didn't look back. "My desire, then, is only to make people believe and know that the ones who have died are still with them, although unseen and unheard, and that They would have those still here to be happy instead of mournful," Marian said.

Marian's first order of business was to take a much-needed vacation to the tropical climate of Guam, where her brother, Lieutenant James Spore, was the acting governor for one year. While she was the guest of honor at parties and balls in Guam, she painted for seven hours a day, every day, until it was time for dinner, dances or a game of cards. James urged his sister to rest and relax, but she couldn't. Her spirit guides urged her to get back to the United States to continue her mission and start her new adventure. She came back from traveling in November and uprooted her life in Michigan to move to the budding and eclectic art mecca of Greenwich Village in New York City in December 1921 at the age of forty-three.

The Psychic Phenomenon

Marian was now fully devoted to painting, and it didn't take long for the New York City media to notice their unusual new resident. Articles describing her ability to paint with the assistance of the dead captured public interest. Back home, the *Bay City Times*, on March 7, 1922, wrote, "Ouija Gives Dr. Flora Spore Correspondence Course in Art," and papers across the United States quickly picked up on her story of "successful dentist turned spirit artist."

The attention quickly earned her a gallery showing in May 1922 at Kingore Gallery in New York City. Her first paintings to ever be publicly displayed were those of exotic and brightly colored temples she had painted while in Guam, surrealistic paintings such as *The Ship of Death*, which showed a billowy-looking white ship flying over a bright blue sea, leaving a trail of white flowers in its wake. Other paintings were of flowers and fruits that looked more like sculptures on a canvas thanks to her use of thickly applied paint to create a bas-relief effect. Her paintings were called "daring" and "imaginative," and while her talent seemed rudimentary, there was something about her style and the feelings the paintings inspired.

Art critics were at a loss for words. If her story was to be believed, here was a woman who had no formal art background or training but was somehow able to quickly create surrealistic paintings that stirred emotions. Her technique and style were unique and refreshing, combined with a bold confidence in the spiritual origin of her abilities. She was dubbed a "psychic phenomenon" by the press. The *Morning Tulsa Daily World*, on May 28, 1922, wrote that her paintings were "fascinating, terrifying, weird and, in spots, horrible. They made one feel as if seeing something in a dream." She would later equate her style of painting and artistic process to "dreaming on canvas."

On June 12, 1922, Anderson Galleries in New York City displayed her work alongside that of other artists who also claimed the hands of spirits controlled their art. The famous author and devoted Spiritualist Sir Arthur Conan Doyle, while on a United States lecture tour, stopped by the gallery to view the art and was impressed with Marian's work.

The paintings on display comprised a series she called the Temple Paintings, which featured vivid colors of gold, blue and scarlet that seemed to jump off the canvas. While the show featured four other spirit artists, Helen B. Wells, Emily Talmadge, Julia Forrest and Frederick Lewis Thompson, it was Marian's work that stole the show. The exhibition was so popular that the gallery was urged to extend the show for another week and remain open

Miss Flora Marian Spore, painting one of her spirit photographs

Left: A newspaper image from the *Evening Journal* (Wilmington), February 16, 1923. *Public domain.*

Right: A newspaper image from the *Bisbee Daily Review*, March 26, 1922. *Public domain.*

later than normal. Over four hundred people a day came to gaze at the art "done by the hands of ghosts." The gallery was filled with people talking about their own experiences with the paranormal, and the *Brooklyn Daily Eagle* wrote that the Anderson Gallery was currently "the spookiest place New York City has ever boasted." The exhibition earned national and even international attention, with two correspondents from a London journal arriving for the opening.

Dr. Hereward Carrington, who had just opened one of the first parapsychological laboratories in the United States in 1921 under the name the American Psychical Institute, suggested, "These so-called spirit-directed paintings are merely expressions of the subconscious mind. The expression comes from that layer of the ego where insanity lurks." Annoyed and angered, Marian told the press she was ready to meet Dr. Carrington at any time to prove him wrong. Carrington was a paranormal explorer who investigated some of the most famous mediums of the early twentieth century, including Eusapia Paladino and Margery Crandon. He supported both women's abilities, even though there was major evidence of trickery surrounding them.

With Marian then living in New York City, Dr. Prince was able to study her more and would bring people to her studio to observe her as she painted.

When she was ready for more instruction from "Them" while painting, she would just tap her paintbrush on the side of her palette, and a conversation would happen immediately. When she wasn't painting and wanted to connect, she would cross her arms and tap her left arm lightly with the fingers of her right hand. "I always feel a slight sensation of cold just before they communicate," she told the *Brooklyn Daily Eagle*. "They seem to see the universe spread out before them in pictures. They describe the future or what They want me to paint. They do it sometimes by thought transference, sometimes by words."

Dr. Prince stated in the *Seattle Daily Times* on August 13, 1922:

> *I respect her for an honest and temperamental red-headed phenomenon and the most thoroughly practical person I have ever seen. From any point of view, her work is worthy of the attention of psychologists, who now neglect her because of their inverted superstitious fear of being involved in something occult. I have watched her paint a picture from start to finish, and I have purposely engaged her in conversation and got her to turn her face away from the canvas while her hand moved swiftly from one point to another. The work had all the appearance, and I am convinced it is so, of being automatic so far as her volition is concerned. What the subconscious mind is doing, I don't know. If it is instigated from the other side, that will be interesting, too. Miss Spore shows peculiar powers that are hard to explain.*

Dr. Prince had planned to write a book about Marian. He studied her for at least two hours a week for two years. He believed in her honesty and had no doubts about her ability. He felt she was "directed by "super-normal intelligences," but unfortunately, his book was never written. He parted ways with the ASPR over its support of medium Margery Crandon, who was being tested in 1922 as part of a cash prize offered by the publication *Scientific American* to find a "genuine medium." Dr. Prince believed Margery to be a fake and formed the Boston Society for Psychical Research in May 1925, which eventually dissolved back into the ASPR by 1941, a few years after Dr. Prince's death in 1934.

The Angel of the Bowery

In 1927, Marian read about two men freezing to death in the Bowery District, a part of New York City with many downtrodden and homeless people.

This didn't sit right with her. She felt no person in a country as wealthy as the United States should freeze to death on the streets. She went to a bank, cashed in a ten-dollar bill for quarters and headed to the Bowery, handing out the quarters to anyone who looked like they could use the money. Feeling like she could do more, she went home and formed a plan, starting with making tickets from colored paper that could get a person a hot meal at the local YMCA, clothing or a place to sleep for the night. If just a few of these people could attain some type of comfort in their life, maybe it could help lift their spirits and get them on a better path.

On Monday and Thursday afternoons, January through April, rain or snow, Marian stood at the head of a line of needy people that extended entire city blocks. She called it "the great mission of her life." Many of the men in line were seasonal workers, and when construction stopped during the winter, so did their work and paychecks. The police even stepped in to help organize the line and point out certain people they knew were worth a little extra charity or, in some cases, someone to avoid helping. Marian would listen to and assess each person in line to decide what would benefit them most. If Marian caught wind that someone took their ticket and traded it for drugs or alcohol, they never received her help again. As her work continued, her donations also included glasses, shoes, wheelchairs, artificial limbs and the occasional train fare to get someone back home to their family.

She kept her identity hidden for three years, not wanting any attention, because it wasn't about her, it was about the needy people. To the public, she was known as the "Angel of the Bowery," or "Lady Bountiful," until a *New York Times* article on February 21, 1930, revealed her identity. "They've called her the mystery woman of the Bowery for the past three years—this titian-haired woman with piercing brown eyes and a ready smile who dispenses charity single-handed on a prodigious scale," wrote the *Brooklyn Daily Eagle*. She was irritated that her cover had been blown. On average, she distributed 1,300 meal tickets a week, 35,000 for an entire season. She made her purchases under the name "The Bowery Foundation" to keep her spending anonymous. Over three years, she gave away an estimated $120,000, over $1.2 million today. The money initially came out of her own pocket. Marian had been smart with the money she made with her dental practice and invested in some successful stocks that greatly paid off just before the Great Depression. Friends also donated to her charitable efforts, including one of her most wealthy friends, Irving T. Bush.

Irving T. Bush

An image of Irving T. Bush.
Courtesy of the Library of Congress.

Within one week of Marian being exposed as "Lady Bountiful," it was reported that Irving T. Bush, the Brooklyn industrial tycoon, owner of the Bush Terminal Company and millionaire, had checked into a hotel in Reno to seek a divorce from his second wife, Maude Howard Beard Bush, and intended to marry Marian Spore. Marian and Irving met in 1927. They lived in the same luxury Park Avenue apartment building, and Irving loved and collected art. He was immediately charmed by Marian when he met her. She was an intelligent and energetic force who wasn't like any other woman he had ever met. Married since 1907, he and his wife had been estranged for some time. Aside from the children they had together, they had nothing else in common anymore.

Reno was known as the "divorce capital of the world," and all one had to do was establish a six-week residency there before a divorce could be granted (unlike in other states, where the divorce process was lengthy or next to impossible). In Reno, there was no need to prove the circumstances for the separation, and the tiny city was also known to keep the press away, affording added privacy for celebrities and the wealthy. After some back and forth between Irving and Maude's lawyers, the divorce was granted on June 9, 1930. One hour later, Irving went to the Reno County clerk, got a marriage license and married the woman he would later say "was the most remarkable person I have ever known."

In 1931, Marian was back at the head of her breadline, only this time, her husband, with "coat off and sleeves rolled up," was sometimes by her side. This was the fourth year of her charity, but other organizations had picked up the torch and were following in Marian's footsteps. There were then eighty-six breadlines operating in the city. She felt like her mission had made a real impact.

THE SHOW MUST GO ON

Marian's first exhibition since her marriage was held at one of the oldest and most conservative locations, the Knoedler Galleries at 13 East Fifty-Seventh Street, and ran from February 6 to 18, 1933, featuring ten new paintings. Marian's style was then heralded as "spontaneous subconscious art," and the press was moving away from the idea of spirit-directed art. Psychologists began showing an interest in her paintings, feeling they were influenced by her subconscious mind, rather than unseen beings in another realm.

TIME magazine reported on the show and noted that her age was "fortyish," but she was fifty-four and had always looked unusually young her whole life. Irving Bush was quoted as saying "he didn't understand" the art but was "beginning to like some of the things in spite of myself." In 1934, her art was shown at the Wildenstein Galleries, and she shocked people with her "unheard-of use of black and white oils." Irving had a home in London, so the pair often spent time there. She would paint and he would tend to his business. Her paintings were exhibited at the fine art galleries on London's Bond Street in 1935, and the conservative British art critics hailed her use of color and design.

A painting by Marian Spore Bush titled *The Gaunt Bird of Famine.* © *Peter A. Juley & Son Collection, Smithsonian American Art Museum.*

PREDICTING THE FUTURE

In 1923, Josephine Van De Grift, a *Buffalo Times* staff writer, interviewed Marian at her Greenwich Village studio and wondered if her guides could predict future events. Marian never went into a trance, the lights were never dimmed; she just sat in her "smock and knickers" and "high-heeled satin pumps" and gave a moment of silence before each question. Many of the questions the reporter asked dealt with post–World War I issues and worries. A few of the questions were:

Josephine: Will Germany turn Bolshevik?
Marian: Germany already has taken up thoughts from the far north. She will use these thoughts to bind herself closer, but she will remain always separate. She will never be a monarchy again. She will always be ruled by many people instead of one.
Josephine: What part will the Orient play in world affairs?
Marian: Japan will play a large part. China will rise. She will be one of the strongest nations of the world. In the end, she will dominate by her wisdom. Japan will hold on by military strength rather than by brains. She will always have to be reckoned with.
Josephine: Will a world leader arise?
Marian: There will be no one leader. There will never be universal peace. Each nation must protect itself. The one best protected will lead.
Josephine: Is there any possibility of a British-French War?
Marian: France already hates England, but the war that is coming will be a world war.

Marian predicted President Harding's sudden death on August 2, 1923. When she made the prediction, she wrote it down and dated it with witnesses present. She often talked about a horrible second world war brewing that would be far more damaging than the first one. In May 1925, Marian said Mayor Hylan of New York City would be defeated, which didn't make Hylan or his friends very happy. He was, in fact, defeated by state senator James "Jimmy" Walker in 1925. One of the eeriest predictions wasn't even given during her interviews but would be more recognizable to anyone living in the twenty-first century. A black-and-white oil painting she created in 1943 shows skyscrapers in New York City with a large explosion and fire. Two black airplanes are flying over the devastation. Had she seen the terrible events of September 11, 2001, back in 1943? The painting was simply named *When?*

An image of Marian Spore Bush admiring one of her large paintings, circa the 1930s. ©
Peter A. Juley & Son Collection, Smithsonian American Art Museum.

Marian wasn't thrilled about giving predictions, because she felt it was
"sensational and showy," plus she found that a lot of people constantly
asked her to tell them about their future. Marian never considered herself
a medium and abhorred Spiritualism, stating, "All of my life, I have hated
Spiritualism with its dark rooms and its mediums and all of that. You can

tell to look at me that I am a sane, practical, everyday person. And I want people to know that I am not a fake, because I am convinced that we all may have access to sources of help that will transform our lives." She further said, "I do not believe in dark rooms, spirit cabinets, megaphones, physical manifestations, ectoplasms or any of the rest of the séance. I do believe that spirits show themselves infrequently, but they can no more be photographed than thought can be."

One of the biggest skeptics of mediumship was the magician Harry Houdini, who Marian knew very well. Houdini said Marian "had something beautiful to give to the world" with her painting, but both of them shared a hatred for the antics that fake mediums and less-genuine Spiritualists did in darkened séance rooms. Marian remembered the mediums back in Bay City and said, "They lived in back streets and told fortunes and were arrested for drunkenness." It bothered Marian that Sir Arthur Conan Doyle had the audacity to suggest Houdini was in fact a real spirit medium and Spiritualist. "He was a great man, a genius, but not a Spiritualist," she said. "I told him once of a remark I had heard that he did his marvelous tricks with the aid of spirits, and he replied that this was his life's work and to have people give credit for it to spirits was 'terrible.'"

May 20, 1943, was the date of Marian's last public exhibition while she was living, which was held again at the Grand Central Art Galleries and titled *Memory and Prophecy*. The exhibition benefited the Red Cross. The paintings were dramatic and featured some of her more bleak and disturbing images that seemed to have warnings of the future imbedded in the very paint strokes. One of the more striking paintings on display was *The Gaunt Bird of Famine*, which shows a sickly-looking white bird flying through a black sky over what looks like an abandoned and ruined city. Other paintings were titled *The Avenger* and *World Aflame*. Marian passed away at the age of sixty-eight on February 24, 1946, at her home. Her obituary in the *New York Times* was ended with a quote from her friend Dr. Walter Franklin Prince: "She represents very unusual and remarkable phenomena, at least part of which is quite beyond explanation by our present science. Her honesty and general character are beyond doubt. That she is able to state facts probably unknown to her to a degree beyond the limits of chance has been absolutely proved to me. Here is a remarkable and perplexing case."

BIBLIOGRAPHY

The Rise of Spiritualism in Michigan

Ann Arbor News. "Ouija Board Talk Draws Big Crowd on Campus Sunday." August 2, 1920.

Britten, Emma Hardinge. *Nineteenth Century Miracles; or, Spirits and Their Work in Every Country on the Earth. A Complete Historical Compendium of the Great Movement Known as "Modern Spiritualism."* New York: William Britten, 1884.

Buckley, Nick. "The Rise and Fall of Harmonia, a Spiritualist Utopia and Home to Sojourner Truth." *Battle Creek Enquirer*, January 9, 2020. https://www.battlecreekenquirer.com/story/life/2019/01/16/rise-and-fall-harmonia-battle-creeks-Spiritualist-utopia/2214809002/.

Grand Rapids Herald. "Here for a Month." July 2, 1899.

———. "In a Tented Village." July 4, 1899.

———. "Keep Away from Ouija Advises Dr. Knudson." March 1, 1920.

Jackson Citizen Patriot. "Ouija Fans!" February 17, 1920.

———. "Vamping Little Ouija." February 15, 1920.

Kansas City Star. "Declare Ouija a Menace." January 19, 1920.

Massie, Larry B. *The Romance of Michigan's Past.* Allegan, MI: Priscilla Press, 1991.

Massie, Larry B., and Peter J. Schmitt. *Battle Creek.* Woodland Hills, CA: Windsor Publications, 1984.

McGarry, Molly. *Ghosts of Futures Past: Spiritualism and the Cultural Politics of Nineteenth-Century America.* Berkeley: University of California Press, 2008.

Melton, J. Gordon, ed. *Encyclopedia of Occultism and Parapsychology*. Vol. 2. 5th ed. Farmington Hills, MI: Gale Group, 2001.

Plain Dealer (Cleveland). "Ouija Boards Said to Replace Bibles." March 9, 1920.

Rodrigues McRobbie, Linda. "The Strange and Mysterious History of the Ouija Board." Smithsonian Institution, October 27, 2013. https://www.

smithsonianmag.com/history/the-strange-and-mysterious-history-of-the-ouija-board-5860627/.

Schneider, Dr. Arle. *A Tale of One Village: Vicksburg, Michigan 1831–2000*. Vicksburg, MI: Vicksburg Historical Society, 2004.

"Spiritualism in Southwest Michigan: Voices from the Great Beyond." *Museography* 1, no. 5 (Fall 2005): 10–11.

Times Herald. "Ouija Board Is a Menace." February 9, 1920.

Tulsa World. "Ouija Is Lure to the Students." January 26, 1920.

The Marvelous Manifestations of Farmer Riley

Chicago Chronicle. "Protest from a Spiritualist." January 26, 1897.

Chicago Tribune. "A Michigan Farmer's Powers." February 26, 1892.

Daily Telegram. "J.D. Hagaman Tells the Story of His Work at Marcellus." June 15, 1894.

———. "State News." August 28, 1894.

Detroit Free Press. "Farmer Riley's Spooks." July 5, 1893.

Flint Journal. "Farmer Medium Is Dead at Marcellus." May 21, 1919.

Flower, Sydney. *The Mediumship of Famer Riley*. Cleveland, OH: Tom Clifford, 1900.

Jones, Lloyd Kenyon, ed. "The Life of James 'Farmer' Riley." *Communication* 1, no. 3 (May 1920): 30

Kalamazoo Gazette. "From Spirit Land." October 15, 1893.

———. "Spooks in Daylight." March 22, 1892.

Muskegon Chronicle. "Closing Meeting Tonight." July 16, 1894.

Mysteries of the Séance and Tricks and Traps of Bogus Mediums. Boston: Lunt Publishers, 1903.

Payne, Laura B., ed. "Sydney Flower, L.L.D., Editor of Suggestive Therapeutics." *Psychic Century* 4, no. 1 (January 31, 1901): 1.

Price, Harry, and Eric J. Dingwall, eds. *Revelations of a Spirit Medium*. New York: E.P. Dutton & Co., 1922.

Saginaw News. "Evening with Spooks." August 8, 1894.

Times Herald. "A Challenge." June 5, 1895.

Vlerebome, Abraham. *The Life of James Riley*. Akron, OH: Werner Company, 1911.

Choose Your Own Coffin

Ann Arbor Daily Times. "The Guardian Angel Told Woman to Take Poison." January 31, 1906.

Flint Journal. "It Puzzles Police." January 30, 1906.

Grand Rapids Press. "Cremate My Body." January 30, 1906.

———. "Defense Is Begun." September 26, 1906.

———. "Drop Spencer Case." September 16, 1907.

———. "Float Over City." February 1, 1906.

———. "Hearing Is Delayed." February 2, 1906.

———. "Is Only a Medium." September 28, 1906.

———. "Jury Is Secured." September 19, 1906.

———. "Leave It to the Courts." February 5, 1906.

———. "Medium in Court." September 17, 1906.

———. "Medium Is Held." March 9, 1906.

———. "Medium Locked Up." January 29, 1906.

———. "Now with Jury." October 2, 1906.

———. "Old Case Dropped." January 1, 1909.

———. "One of the Sixteen." May 23, 1906.

———. "Realm of Spirits." September 27, 1906.

———. "Seeking a Jury." September 18, 1906.

———. "She Is Not Insane." February 6, 1906.

———. "Some Queer Facts." September 21, 1906.

———. "Spencer Case On." February 21, 1906.

———. "Spencer Case On." March 7, 1906.

———. "Spirits' Haunt Is Sold." March 5, 1906.

———. "Sturgis on Stand." February 22, 1906.

———. "Tells of Spirits." February 9, 1906.

———. "Told Weird Tale." September 20, 1906.

———. "Trial of Trance Medium Begun at Grand Rapids." September 20, 1906.

———. "Was Under Spell." September 25, 1906.

Kalamazoo Gazette. "Prayers and Fits Are Her Methods." September 28, 1906.

The "Devilish Cunningness" of Edward Ascher

Courier-Journal (Louisville). "Lang the Mediums." September 19, 1897.

———. "Medium Lang Dismissed." September 23, 1897.

———. "Strange Drink." September 18, 1897.

———. "Taken Under Advisement." September 22, 1897.

Detroit Free Press. "An Alibi for Ascher." April 17, 1903.

———. "Another Analysis." August 31, 1898.

———. "Arraign Ascher Today." August 27, 1898.

———. "Ascher after Pardon." November 15, 1904.

———. "Ascher at Ease." September 3, 1898.

———. "Ascher Case Went Over." November 14, 1901.

———. "Ascher Goes to Jackson." April 25, 1899.

———. "Ascher, Hayes, Holzhay, Are Freed by Warner." December 31, 1910.

———. "Ascher Is Held." August 24, 1898.

———. "Ascher Jury Discharged." November 17, 1901.

———. "Ascher Jury out at 3 a.m." April 25, 1903.

———. "Ascher Jury Secured." November 5, 1901.

———. "Ascher Not to Have Freedom." December 10, 1904.

———. "Ascher's Alibi." August 21, 1898.

———. "Ascher's Defense." April 19, 1899.

———. "Ascher's Favorite Charm." April 14, 1899.

———. "Ascher's Romance." April 16, 1899.

———. "Ascher's Second Trial." March 16, 1899.

———. "Ascher Still Has Hopes." April 27, 1903.

———. "Ascher Testimony Rehashed." April 12, 1899.

———. "Ascher Trial Next Week." February 13, 1903.

———. "Ascher Was Given Several Presents." April 29, 1903.

———. "Ascher Was the Man." August 23, 1898.

———. "Broke Down in Court." April 1, 1903.

———. "Didn't Proceed Far." December 13, 1898.

———. "End of the Ascher Case." April 20, 1899.

———. "Faced the Defendant." December 20, 1898.

———. "For Life." April 25, 1899.

———. "Go to Jury Thursday." April 19, 1903.

———. "Judge Murphy Upheld." May 20, 1902.

———. "The Jury Disagreed." December 25, 1898.

———. "Jury Has Agreed!" April 23, 1899.

———. "Jury Out." December 25, 1898.

———. "Lieutenant Was Accused." March 22, 1903.

———. "Life Sentence for Ed Ascher." April 26, 1903.

———. "Must Stand Trial." September 10, 1898.

———. "The Net that Held Ascher." April 24, 1899.

———. "Nine Men for Ascher Jury." February 26, 1903.

———. "Poison or Drowning?" December 16, 1898.

———. "Powerful Plea for Ascher." April 22, 1899.

———. "Prosecution Rested." September 7, 1898.

———. "Swindler, Liar, Cheat, Scoundrel." April 21, 1899.

———. "Theory of Defense." March 31, 1903.

———. "Twelve Men Tried and True." April 11, 1899.

———. "Two French Women." January 18, 1899.

———. "Two More Witnesses." December 21, 1898.

———. "Weighted with Stones." August 19, 1898.

———. "With Devilish Cunningness." August 20, 1898.

———. "Without a Witness." December 23, 1898.

———. "Witnesses Have Scattered." May 27, 1901.

Jackson Citizen Patriot. "The Nichols Murder." August 20, 1898.

———. "Probable Murder." August 23, 1898.

Consulting Spirits: The Strange Finale of Eber B. Ward

Chaney, H.A., and Hoyt Post, eds. *The Michigan Lawyer*. Detroit, MI: Richmond, Backus and Co., 1875.

Daisy, Michael. "The Captain of Everything: Eber Brock Ward." *Mostly Detroit*, April 5, 2013. http://mostlydetroit.blogspot.com/2013/04/the-captain-of-everything-eber-brock.html.

Detroit Free Press. "Atrocious Conduct of a Steamboat Captain." October 8, 1862.

———. "Bloody Tragedy." October 16, 1865.

———. "Captain E.B. Ward Funeral." January 7, 1875.

———. "Captain E.B. Ward Last Will and Testament." January 8, 1875.

———. "Death of Captain E.B. Ward." January 3, 1875.

———. "Death of Milton D. Ward." August 1, 1877.

———. "John P. Ward in a New Role." September 13, 1865.

———. "The Murder Trial." November 16, 1867.

———. "The Murder Trial." November 17, 1867.

———. "The Murder Trial." November 18, 1867.

———. "The Murder Trial." November 19, 1867.

———. "The Murder Trial." November 20, 1867.

———. "Trial for Murder." November 15, 1867.

———. "Ward's Will." September 22–November 13, 1875.

———. "The Ward Will." March 24, 1875.

———. "Wayne Circuit Court." November 20, 1867.

Donovan, J.W. *Modern Jury Trials and Advocates*. New York: Banks and Brothers, 1882.

Guiley, Rosemary E. *The Encyclopedia of Ghosts and Spirits*. New York: Checkmark Books, 2000.

Hillsdale Standard. "The Death of Captain Ward." October 31, 1865.

New York Times. "The Attempt to Break E.B. Ward's Will." March 15, 1875.

Passante, Anna. "Eber Brock Ward, Midwest Captain of Industry." *Bay View Compass*, July 1, 2010. https://bayviewcompass.com/eber-brock-ward-midwest-captain-of-industry/.

Tompert, Ann, ed. *The Way Things Were: An Autobiography of Emily Ward*. Marine City, MI: Newport Press, 1976.

Wargo, Justin. "'A Case Without Parallel': The Sensational Battle over Eber Brock Ward's Will and Subsequent Legacy of Detroit's First Great Industrialist." *Michigan Historical Review* 39, no. 2 (2013): 77–103.

The Legend of the Nain Rouge

Brown, Henry D. *Cadillac and the Founding of Detroit*. Detroit, MI: Wayne State University Press, 1976.

Detroit Free Press. "Hamlin Will Retain the Property." August 2, 1892.

———. "Mrs. Marie Caroline Watson-Hamlin." June 23, 1885.

DeVito, Lee. "Raising Nain." *Detroit Metro Times*, March 16, 2016, 32–36.

Hamlin, Marie Caroline Watson. *Legends of Le Detroit*. Detroit, MI: Thorndike Nourse, 1884.

LaForest, James. "M. Caroline Watson Hamlin and Detroit Folklore." *Red Cedar*, March 28, 2013. https://theredcedar.wordpress.com/2013/03/28/marie-caroline-watson-hamlin-detroit-folklore-and-french-canadian-identity/.

Langlois, Janet. "Urban Legends and the Faces of Detroit." In *Michigan Folklife Reader*. Edited by C. Kurt Dewhurst and Yvonne Lockwood. East Lansing: Michigan State University Press, 1987, 107–20.

Langlois, Janet, and Bob MacDonald. "Folklore." *Daily Tribune* (Royal Oak), October 1, 1986, 4.

Lyons, Mickey. *Wicked Detroit*. Charleston, SC: The History Press, 2018.

Pioneer Collections Report of the Pioneer Society of the State of Michigan. Vol. 4. Lansing, MI: W.S. George and Co. Printers and Binders, 1883.

The Lonely Ghost of Minnie Quay

Beck, Earl Clifton. *Lore of the Lumber Camps*. Ann Arbor: University of Michigan Press, 1948.

———. *Songs of the Michigan Lumberjacks*. Ann Arbor: University of Michigan Press, 1941.

Cohen, Norm. *American Folk Songs: A Regional Encyclopedia*. Vol. 2. Westport, CT: Greenwood Press, 2008.

Detroit Free Press. "Thumb Track." June 21, 1988.

DuMond, Neva. *Thumb Diggings*. Lexington, MI: Self-published, 1962.

Kalamazoo Gazette. "State News." April 29, 1876.

Kuclo, Marion. *Michigan Haunts and Hauntings*. Lansing, MI: Thunder Bay Press, 1993.

Portrait and Biographical Album of Sanilac County. Chicago: Chapman Brothers, 1884.

Sanilac Jeffersonian. "Suicide at Forester." April 29, 1876.

Stonehouse, Frederick. *Haunted Lake Huron*. Duluth, MN: Lake Superior Port Cities Inc., 2007.

Times Herald (Port Huron). "Forester Won't Fade Away." March 27, 2004.

———. "The Haunting of Sanilac." April 9, 1990.

———. "The Victim of Slander." May 2, 1876.

Haunted Roads and Mysterious Lights

Detroit Free Press. "Action Line." October 15, 1967.

———. "Action Line." October 31, 1968.

Dorson, Richard M. *American Folklore*. Chicago: University of Chicago Press, 1977.

Dzwonkowski, Ron. "Sprawl May Scare Away the Legendary Denton Road Ghost." *Detroit Free Press*, October 31, 1999.

Godfrey, Linda S. *Weird Michigan*. New York: Sterling Publishing, 2006.

Langlois, Janet. "Urban Legends and the Faces of Detroit." In *Michigan Folklife Reader*. Edited by C. Kurt Dewhurst and Yvonne Lockwood. East Lansing: Michigan State University Press, 1987, 107–20.

Oates, Morgan. "Is that Girl Ghost Still Rattling Slabs?" *Detroit Free Press*, July 16, 1961.

Parker, Virginia Bailey. *Ghost Stories and Other Tales from Canton*. Canton, MI: Canton Historical Society, 1998.

The Jackson Disturbance

Detroit Free Press. "Jackson Bandit Admits Murder." March 2, 1918.

————. "Vicious 'Ghost' Plagues Family." February 3, 1962.

————. "Who Haunted Jackson Home?" October 10, 1963.

Greensboro Daily News. "Report Is Expected in 'Ghost' Case." February 9, 1962.

Ironwood Daily Globe. "House Is Sick, Owner Claims." February 3, 1962.

Lansing State Journal. "Ghosts? Weird Doings Take Place in House at Jackson." February 2, 1962.

————. "Sentenced as Youth, Killer May Be Freed." May 7, 1936.

Lebanon Daily News. "Noisy Ghosts?" February 3, 1962.

News-Palladium. "Likes Living in Ghost House." June 3, 1965.

Racine Journal-Times. "Like to Buy a 'Sick' House?" February 4, 1962.

Roll, William G. *The Poltergeist*. New York: Nelson Doubleday Inc., 1972.

Smith, Leanne. "Peek through Time: Flying Knives, Eerie Sounds Haunted Maltby Street Home in 1961." *MLive*, October 28, 2015. https://www.mlive.com/news/jackson/2015/10/peek_through_time_flying_knive.html.

Taylor, Troy. "The Jackson, Michigan Poltergeist." *Ghosts of the Prairie*, 2002. https://web.archive.org/web/20030814044136/http://www.prairieghosts.com/jack_poltergeist.html.

Terre Haute Tribune. "Poltergeists Invade Home." February 11, 1962.

Times Herald. "Jackson Youth Is Given Life for His Crime." March 2, 1918.

Williams, Bryan J. "The Psychical Research Foundation and Its Legacy Under William G. Roll: Past Findings and Future Directions." Psychical Research Foundation Anniversary/Roll Tribute Paper, 2012. https://www.psychicalresearchfoundation.com.

"Ye Shall See Strange Visions"

Detroit Free Press. "Believed in Witchcraft." February 6, 1910.

————. "No Faith in Witchcraft." April 10, 1910.

————. "Police Guard Girl Said to Be Witch." January 25, 1917.

Flint Journal. "Taken for Witch." March 9, 1910.

Grand Rapids Press. "Detroit Folk Accuse Girl of Witchery." January 25, 1917.

Kansas City Star. "Devil Girl Is Frantic." January 27, 1917.

Wichita Eagle. "A Witch Panic in Detroit." Mary 25, 1917.

Driven Mad by Witchcraft

Detroit Free Press. "Dealing with Witches." August 2, 1884.

————. "Old Salem Revived." July 31, 1884.

————. "The Queer Mt. Morris Bewitching Case." August 1, 1884.

————. "Will Go to the Asylum to Fight the Witches." August 6, 1884.

Lake County Star. "The Mount Morris Witches." August 7, 1884.

St. Louis Globe-Democrat. "Hounded by Witches." August 5, 1884.

Frank Lesner, Witch Killer

Detroit Free Press. "Court Brevities." June 6, 1905.
———. "Four Insane Convicts." September 15, 1908.
———. "Frank Lesner." June 20, 1905.
———. "I'm Glad I Did It." June 21, 1905.
———. "Is Sorry He Did It." May 18, 1905.
———. "Jaunty Air Regained." May 19, 1905.
———. "Lesner Is in High Spirits." May 21, 1905.
———. "Lesner Was Formally Declared a Murderer." May 25, 1905.
———. "Owned Up to Killing His Godmother." May 17, 1905.
———. "Pleaded Guilty." May 20, 1905.
———. "Say Lesner's Insane." June 15, 1905.
Ionia County MIGenWeb. "Michigan State Prisons in Ionia County." January 11, 2008. http://ionia.migenweb.org/history/prisons.htm.
Steuben Republican. "The Case of Daniel Danning." August 27, 1919.
———. "Circuit Court." December 19, 1917.
———. "Daniel Danning." November 20, 1940.
———. "Daniel Danning Granted." November 26, 1919.
———. "Marian Danning." December 20, 1916.
———. "Marian Danning vs. Daniel." February 13, 1918.
———. "Mary Joan Danning." December 20, 1916.

The Devil in Detroit

Detroit Free Press. "City's Clerks Must Be Busy." September 26, 1906.
———. "Devil and Giant." May 30, 1948.
———. "Devil Hides Horns." November 12, 1905.
———. "Devil Must Fall." November 9, 1905.
———. "The Devil Statue." November 10, 1905.
———. "Here's a Thing to Conjure Menz Will Raise Devil." September 24, 1908.
———. "Herman Menz Will Not Take Court Oath in Usual Form." November 28, 1916.
———. "Hoodoo Devil Expelled from Electric Park." June 15, 1908.
———. "Menz Has a Permit." November 14, 1905.
———. "Menz Raises Devil Again." November 2, 1908.
———. "Menz's Devil Is on Exhibition as a Show Freak." November 13, 1905.
———. "Menz's Devil Not Alone." November 11, 1905.
———. "Menz Will Shoot." December 31, 1905.
———. "Revival Booms." November 9, 1905.
———. "Spirit of Riot." November 10, 1905.
———. "To Sell the Devil." December 27, 1905.
Hutchens, Kate. "A Monument to Satan; Menz's Teufel." *Scapegoat* (Summer/ Autumn 2013): 388–93.

Stark, George W. *In Old Detroit.* Chicago: Arnold-Powers Inc., 1939.

"A Statue Erected to the Devil." *Public Opinion: A Comprehensive Summary of the Press Throughout the World on All Important Current Topics* (July–December 1905): 696.

The Summer of the Monster

Bord, Colin, and Janet Bord. *Bigfoot Casebook Updated: Sightings and Encounters from 1818 to 2004.* N.p: Pine Winds Press, 2006.

Cutchin, Joshua, and Timothy Renner. *Where the Footprints End: High Strangeness and the Bigfoot Phenomenon.* Vol. 2. *Evidence.* N.p: Self-published, 2020.

Detroit Free Press. "Beast Town Booms." June 13, 1964.

Escanaba Daily Press. "Clare Brothers See Monster." June 17, 1964.

———. "Sister Lakes Monster May Be Big Bear." June 13, 1964.

Herald-Press (Saint Joseph). "Girls Report Seeing Monster Early Today!" June 11, 1964.

———. "Monster Hunt Flops." June 11, 1964.

Holland Evening Sentinel. "Cass County Residents Still Remember Monster." October 6, 1964.

———. "Chamber Not Unhappy with Monster." June 13, 1964.

———. "Gas Stations Offer." June 13, 1964.

———. "Huge Monster Frightens Girls." June 11, 1964.

———. "Hunt Monster in Ionia County." June 17, 1964.

Ironwood Daily Globe. "Migrants Leave, Fearing Monster." June 15, 1964.

Lansing State Journal. "Report Monster at Ionia." June 17, 1964.

News-Palladium (Benton Harbor). "Girls Say They Saw Monster." June 11, 1964.

———. "Monster Goes on Vacation." June 15, 1964.

———. "Monster Is Huge and Hairy." June 11, 1964.

———. "Monster Reported Near Sister Lakes." June 10, 1964.

———. "Offers, Withdraws $1000 Monster Reward." June 13, 1964.

———. "State Trooper Sees Monster." June 18, 1964.

———. "Ten People (But Not Deputies) See Monster." June 12, 1964.

Raleigh Register. "Monster James Michigan Traffic." June 11, 1964.

South Bend Tribune. "Hairy Monster Scare Lessens." June 14, 1964.

True Magazine. "The Hellzapoppin' Hunt for the Michigan Monster." June 1966.

The Mysterious Life and Times of Marian Spore Bush

Bay City Times. "At the University." May 23, 1898.

———. "Flora M. Spore, Dentist." March 11, 1900.

———. "Miss Spore's Western Trip." June 27, 1921.

———. "Practice Dentistry." April 4, 1899.

Bay County Historical Society. *Women of Bay County.* Saginaw, MI: Acorn Press, 1980.

Boston Herald. "Psychic Predicts Defeat of Hylan." May 9, 1925.

Brooklyn Daily Eagle. "Becomes Pet of Unseen Group." February 5, 1928.

———. "Hunches and Not Spirits Guide Her Painting." January 31, 1933.

———. "Is This Girl Painter Fake or Psychic?" November 23, 1924.

———. "Medium Who Knew Houdini Calls Him Genius." November 25, 1927.

———. "Messages from Dead." December 3, 1924.

———. "Miss Spore's Spirit Painting of Siamese Temple Exhibited." June 16, 1922.

———. "Mrs. Bush Dreams on Canvas." March 25, 1938.

———. "Reveal Bowery Angel as Spirit Painter." February 25, 1930.

———. "Something New at the Kingore Gallery." May 7, 1922.

Bush, Marian Spore. *They.* New York: Beechhurst Press, 1947.

Columbus (GA) *Daily Enquirer.* "Women May Aid Families and Nation." December 6, 1931.

Daily Illinois State Journal. "Ghost of Dore Guides My Hand, Artist Says." March 19, 1922.

Daily Illinois State Register. "Spiritualist Oil Pictures Puzzle N.Y. Art Critics." June 13, 1922.

Daily News (New York). "Lady Bountiful Goes West." March 23, 1930.

Denver Post. "Ghosts Guide Girl Artist's Hand." August 9, 1922.

Detroit Free Press. "Girl Foretold Harding's End." August 12, 1923.

Evening Journal (Wilmington). "An Interview with the Spirits." February 16, 1923.

Lexington Herald. "Ghosts Guide Painter's Hand." March 18, 1922.

Los Angeles Times. "'They' Guide Artist's Hand." May 23, 1943.

Modesto Evening News. "Mystic Paintings." June 14, 1922.

Morning Tulsa Daily World. "Critics Amazed by Spirit Art of Gotham Girl." May 28, 1922.

New York Times. "Irving T. Bush Weds Miss Marian Spore in Reno." June 10, 1930.

———. "Mrs. Irving Bush, Unusual Artist." February 25, 1946.

———. "New Lady Bountiful Aiding the Bowery." February 21, 1930.

———. "Put Spook Pictures on at Anderson's." June 10, 1922.

Omaha World Herald. "Spirit Stuff." June 6, 1943.

Saginaw News. "Dr. Flora M. Spore." August 5, 1899.

San Diego Union. "Big Business, Astral Angel and Romance." August 3, 1930.

San Francisco Chronicle. "Ghosts Guide the Hands that Make These Pictures." July 23, 1922.

Seattle Daily Times. "Spirits of Dead Masters." August 13, 1922.

Sioux City Journal. "Bush Is in Reno." February 27, 1930.

Spore, Marian. "My Work on the Bowery." *North American Review*, August 1930.

Springfield Sunday Republican. "Do Spirits Guide Her Artistic Hand?" September 14, 1924.

State Times Advocate (Baton Rouge). "Wealthy Bride Gives Away Meal Tickets." January 10, 1931.

TIME. "Art: Automatic Painting." February 20, 1933.

———. "Prophetess." June 7, 1943.

ABOUT THE AUTHOR

For over twenty years, Amberrose Hammond has been researching the supernatural, weird and off-beat history of Michigan. An avid local history and cemetery enthusiast, Amberrose has lectured extensively around the state at libraries, conferences and historical cemetery tours and has shared her love of Michigan's weird side with thousands. She is the author of *Ghosts & Legends of Michigan's West Coast*, *Wicked Ottawa County* and *Wicked Grand Rapids*. Learn more at www.michigansotherside.com and www.amberrosehammond.com, and search and listen to *Ghostly Talk*, a podcast she is a cohost of.